MentalRules®
for Golf

MentalRules®
for Golf

61 Innovative Strategies for Unleashing Your Golf Potential

GREGG M. STEINBERG, Ph.D.

TowleHouse Publishing
Nashville, Tennessee

TowleHouse books are distributed by National Book Network (NBN), 4720 Boston Way, Lanham, Maryland 20706.

Library of Congress Cataloging-in-Publication Data

Steinberg, Gregg M., 1963–.
  Mentalrules for golf : 61 innovative strategies for unleashing your golf potential / Gregg M. Steinberg.
     p. cm.
Includes bibliographical references.
  ISBN 1-931249-22-9 (alk. paper)
  1. Golf--Psychological aspects. 2. Golf. I. Title: Mental rules for golf.
II. Title: 61 innovative strategies for unleashing your golf potential. IV. Title.

  GV979.P75 S84 2003
  796.352'01'9--dc21

                                                             2002155558

Cover design by Gore Studio, Inc.
Page design by Mike Towle

Printed in the United States of America
1 2 3 4 5 6 — 07 06 05 04 03

Contents

*To all golfers throughout the world who want
to improve their mental game:*

*Find your passion
Create your path
Make the commitment
Enjoy the journey*

Introduction

"Compared to what we ought to be, we are only half awake. The human individual lives far within its limits. He possesses powers of various sorts which he habitually fails to use."[1]

—William James

Only a few golfers have ever truly mastered the mental secrets of success under tournament pressure. Bobby Jones, Ben Hogan, Jack Nicklaus, Tom Watson, Annika Sorenstam, and Tiger Woods are among those who come to mind. When the tournament is on the line, they can think their way to victory. They have learned to heat up their talent in competitive situations. On the other hand, many other golfers with immense physical ability have never fully realized their potential. When the heat is on, their games remain frozen.

What allows some golfers to stand tall under tournament pressure while others succumb to the moment? Visualize two cans of soda, one empty and one full. These cans represent two different golfers exposed to tournament conditions. Competitive pressure produces intense forces such as fear of failure, avoidance of big mistakes, a desire to post a good score for friends and family, and the ability to focus when the adrenaline is flowing. Picture grasping the empty can, with your hand being analogous to the forces of tournament play. If nothing is inside the can, these forces will easily crush it. Likewise, if you do not have the requisite mental skills to withstand the pressure of competition, you will cave in. Now, visualize the full can of soda in your hand. No matter how hard you squeeze, this can cannot be crushed. Successful golfers who are filled with great mental skills don't fold under the pressure of championship golf.

MentalRules® for Golf gives you the mental ingredients essential to handling the pressures of golf. This book gives you more than just vital knowledge about the mental game, however. Learning is an active process; therefore, activities and applied experiences are woven into each rule, or lesson, to place you on the path to better thinking.

Let this book awaken your dormant and untapped resources. Every strategy can be used as a daily refresher course for improving your mental approach to assist in unleashing your golfing potential.

Wear the Red Shirt

"I have always thought that the actions of men are the best interpreters of their thoughts."[2]

—John Locke

We all have seen Tiger Woods wear his red shirt when in contention on Sunday, but why did he adopt this behavior? It's a matter of purpose. Woods feels more aggressive when he wears his red shirt. He knows he must play aggressively on Sunday if he is to go "low" and win.

The key question: How does wearing a red shirt make Woods feel more aggressive on the golf course? More important, how can *his* red shirt help *your* golf game?

First, the color red represents aggression and assertiveness. Consider the matador, who uses a red cape to entice the bull to charge at him.

Second, according to self-perception theory, we infer our emotions from our actions. Our brain gets the message from our body how to feel.[3] When we smile, we infer that we are happy because we our smiling. Even faking a smile will make us happier. Likewise, wearing red helps convince Woods to feel and act more aggressive in his pursuit of going low.

The principle of Woods's red shirt can have a huge impact on your confidence level. One way to become more confident is by simply acting confident. Walking off the green with shoulders slumped and head down after missing an easy putt makes a golfer feel less confident in subsequent holes. On the other hand, a golfer fresh off a double bogey can maintain his confidence by keeping his chin up, literally.

If you want to feel more aggressive on the golf course, wear the red shirt. If you want more confidence, strut your stuff all the time, no matter what. If you want to have more fun, just keep on smiling.

2

Go with Whom You Brought to the Dance

"Once you have your practice and you have your mechanics, you must be able to walk out there and trust your mechanics." [4]

—**Aaron Baddeley**

Mac O'Grady is one kind of golf genius. He is a teaching guru to some tour professionals and an expert on golf swing mechanics. O'Grady also is an incredibly talented player. He has won on the PGA Tour and can play scratch golf from both sides of the ball. O'Grady's talent also allowed him to copy many of the great swingers of his day such as Lee Trevino, Johnny Miller, and Jack Nicklaus. He mentioned that he would use a different swing dependent on his mood or the demands of the shot.

Unfortunately, it appears that O'Grady's mind got in the way of his great talent. He had so many different types

3

of swings and so many different types of swing thoughts that he probably got confused when it came to simply trusting his instincts and sticking with his own swing.

O'Grady has plenty of company, and they number in the millions. When playing well, golfers typically will stick with one or two main swing thoughts. However, when things go awry, golfers search for answers. They stop trusting their swings and swing thoughts. They will switch to any idea that might work. It is as if they are switching partners in the middle of the dance.

What usually happens when you switch partners at the dance? You get slapped in the face. The same happens to you when you keep switching swing thoughts in the middle of a round. You lose confidence in your ability and you simply get confused about what you must do out there. When this happens, the course will slap you right in the face.

It's all about trust.

Believing Is Seeing

"Man is what he believes."

—**Anton Chekov**

O ur belief system can change our physiology. Medical research has documented time and again how patients feel better when given an inert substance such as a sugar pill, if they are told that this pill will be beneficial to their health. They believe in the pill, and it helps their healing process.[5]

Our belief system can even make us superior athletes. One great example is Roger Bannister, the first man to finally break the four-minute mile. However, within the next eighteen months, forty-five other runners quickly followed Bannister in breaking that once "impenetrable" mark. After watching Bannister break that barrier, those runners now believed they also could run that fast.[6]

Your belief system can also create great performances on the golf course. Francis Bacon once wrote, "The instruments of the mind are as important as the instruments in the hand." The golf clubs will work much more effectively if you believe in your ability to make them work. Presented with a tough shot over water, you must first believe you can accomplish the shot. Positive expectations will keep your muscles relaxed, giving you the extra power needed to clear the hazard.

This same principle goes for breaking the scoring barriers of 80, 90, or 100 for the first time. When most golfers are having the round of their life, they get out of their comfort zone, tense up, have a blow-up hole or two, and ruin their chances. They did not believe they were capable enough to break that scoring barrier. The old saying "Seeing is believing" should be flipped around. Believing is seeing. You must first believe if you want to see it.

6

Embrace the Challenge

"Of all the virtues we can learn, no trait is more useful, more essential for survival, and more likely to improve the quality of life than the ability to transform adversity into an enjoyable challenge." [7]

—**Mihaly Csikszentmihaly**

A variation of the Greek mythological story of Sisyphus illustrates how to transform adversity into an enjoyable challenge. Sisyphus was caught eavesdropping on the gods, and they became very upset with this type of mortal behavior. As punishment, the gods decreed that Sisyphus for all eternity would have to push a large rock up a steep hill until he reached the top. Sisyphus could never reach the top, because the weight of the rock would overcome him, and it would roll back down the hill. Then he would perpetually begin the process all over again.

Sisyphus was very intelligent, though, and he knew that if he enjoyed this eternal challenge, the sentence would go by much more quickly. He decided to take a different approach each time he pushed the rock up the hill. The first time he got a feel for what the rock and the hill were like. The next time he went as fast as he could. The third time he tried to see how gracefully he could push the rock, etc.

At times the game of golf can make you feel like Sisyphus. You might have your swing working for a week or so, only to find that you lose it right before an important tournament. Or, your putting is working beautifully one day, and the next day you wonder what happened to all the magic. Golfers are in the eternal pursuit of pushing their games up a steep hill with hopes of developing consistency and expertise, only to find that their skills have once again slid down the slippery slope.

Rather than seeing the challenge of obtaining expertise in golf as insurmountable, golfers should adopt the Sisyphus mentality. When your chipping goes awry, embrace the opportunity and focus on your putting for that day. If you hit a bad tee shot and are blocked by a tree, do not see the tree as an obstacle but as an opportunity to work on your escape shots. Phil Mickelson takes this approach, saying, "I love being creative and try to make birdies from behind the trees. That is what makes golf fun."[8]

Rocco Mediate also followed the Sisyphus mentality by embracing his own adversity after he injured his back in 1993, after he had climbed into the top twenty on the money list. But Mediate saw his injury as a personal challenge. By investing thousands of hours into rehab and weight workouts, he not only gained a new buff body but a new level of patience and a newfound joy for the game. Mediate had faced adversity but learned to push the rock back up the hill with greater enthusiasm.[9]

Focus on Yourself

"No man (or woman) can make you feel inferior without your consent." [10]
—**Eleanor Roosevelt**

The number-one fear in our culture is public speaking. Our heart rate goes sky high, our head starts to pound, and at times, some of us will forget everything we had prepared. Our greatest fear is to stand in front of others and look like a fool.

This concern can carry over into our golf game and ruin our play. The story of Ian Baker-Finch's career illustrates this point exceptionally well. Baker-Finch won the British Open in 1991, but within seven years of his victory had retired from professional golf, still in his thirties. Many factors contributed to this decision, one being his humiliating open round of 92 at the British Open at Troon. Another was his thirty-two straight missed cuts. Poignantly, he said, "What I would like to be able to do is to change my name, come back in a different body, and go play without the pressure of being Ian Baker-Finch." [11]

Another similar story involves Hale Irwin's playing with a young greenhorn named Mark O'Meara. O'Meara was playing terribly. He was ashamed about how bad he was playing in front of older, more seasoned pros. After the round, he went up to Irwin and apologized for his bad play. Irwin bluntly told O'Meara that he didn't give a damn how his playing partners shoot, only his own play. [12]

Next time you step on the golf course, be like Hale. Focus only on yourself. Don't worry about what other people think: They aren't worried about you, your score, or your herky-jerky swing. They're doing what you should be doing: They're thinking only about themselves and how fantastic they look in their new golf sweater.

11

Zen and the Art of Golf

"I never worry about the future. It will come soon enough."
—Albert Einstein

Phil Jackson is known as the Zen coach of basketball. He drew from Native-American religions and Zen Buddhism to help guide the Chicago Bulls to six world championships and the Los Angeles Lakers to three consecutive titles. One of the main philosophies of Buddhism is staying in the moment. Such a philosophy promotes letting go of all your doubts. That allows us to concentrate all our energies on the task at hand.

Michael Jordan, one of Jackson's former disciples, noted that being purely wrapped up in the moment has allowed him to play basketball without any self-criticism or doubt or inhibition of any kind.[13]

Comparable to Jordan's talent on the basketball court was Bobby Jones's ability on the golf course. Although Jones did not recognize it as a Zen philosophy, he followed the principle of playing for the moment and believed that this was key to his great play. He said, "It is nothing new or original to say that golf is played one stroke at a time. But it took me many years to realize it."[14]

Another all-time great who followed the Zen philosophy was Walter Hagen. While he was known for his flamboyance, Hagen also had a great golfing mind. He knew he was going to miss a lot of shots, but he knew it was essential to focus on the next shot and let go of the past. In words of timeless wisdom, he once said, "If you worry about the ones you missed, you are going to keep missing them."[15]

There are times when golfers lose their Zen. It happened to Michael Campbell, who led the 1995 British Open going into the last day. That Saturday night he lay awake in bed thinking of all the benefits victory would mean to his finances as well as how a win at a major would change his life

13

forever. He focused well ahead of himself and paid the price with a 76 on the final day, finishing third.[16]

There is an old Buddhist saying, "When an individual tries to catch two birds with one stone, he usually ends up not catching any."[17] Focusing on past follies or wishful rewards on future holes decreases the chance of catching any type of bird in the present moment.

The Einstein Factor

"I believe that my creative mind is my greatest weapon." [18]
—**Tiger Woods**

A lbert Einstein had one of the greatest minds the world has ever known. His contributions to science, such as his theory of relativity, changed the future of our world as well as created a new philosophy of our universe.

Many academics have pondered Einstein's genius. Given what we know about the different regions of the brain, Einstein's ability to use both sides of his brain to resolve dilemmas in science may have led to his great genius. The left side of the brain is characterized by analytical thought: Einstein had an incredible grasp of physics that allowed him to understand that the description of the universe was flawed. In contrast, the right side of the brain is characterized by imaginative thought. Einstein could devise, conduct, and analyze the results of the most intricate scientific experiments all within the confines of his incredible mind.[19]

The ability to use both sides of the brain also appears to facilitate golfing performance. In a study conducted at Arizona State University by sport psychologist Debra Crews, golfers were asked to putt under competitive conditions while their brain patterns were monitored. To increase the players' pressure, she told them that the best players would get a $200 reward while the worst performers would have to pay the experimenters $100. Crews found significant differences in brain activity between the best and worst putters. Specifically, the best putters had equal amounts of left- and right-brain activity while the golfers who choked in the study were characterized by excessive left-brain activity.[20]

Typically, most golfers only emphasize the left side of their brain when they play. They analyze the terrain and then decide what shot is needed, focusing on one or two key swing thoughts. Unfortunately, this is where most will stop their mental approach. They end up using only the left side of their brain, which is analogous to playing with a half set of clubs.[21]

If you want to tap into your golfing genius and play with a full mental set, involve the right side of your brain. Think of the course as your canvas and your clubs as your paintbrushes. Each hole is a new painting to be created. Have a clear visualization of the trajectory of your next shot and where you want it to land. Golfing great Jack Nicklaus said he never hit a shot until he had a vivid image in his mind of what he wanted to accomplish. Seve Ballesteros likens his creative powers around the green to hearing tunes being played by his clubs. He understands the notes his clubs are playing, and this allows him to compose the melody needed for each shot.[22]

Dr. Win Wenger, author of *The Einstein Factor*, stated that many geniuses are normal individuals who have developed a technique that promotes a more sophisticated perception of their world.[23] Perhaps the secret to developing your genius on the golf course is to include a vision of creativity into your game.

8

Prepare for Adversity

"I will prepare and some day my chance will come."
—**Abraham Lincoln**

Golf is full of mishaps, from bad bounces to unfortunate lies in the middle of the fairway. Preparing for adverse conditions is a necessity for developing excellence.

Payne Stewart knew this. In many of his practice rounds, he would hit two balls on every shot, then use the worst one each time.[24] Stewart was preparing to play his best from poor conditions. Given that the U.S. Open is full of adverse situations, perhaps this drill is one thing that helped him win two Opens.

Preparation also involves perspiration. Before the 1987 PGA Championship, held in Florida, Nick Faldo prepared for Florida's heat and high humidity by sitting in a sauna regularly for three weeks prior to the tournament.[25]

An excellent method to prepare for adverse conditions is with the development of an adversity plan. This plan is a composite of strategies for dealing with difficulties on the course. For instance, most tournaments are played at a snail's pace. One strategy in the plan would be to always respond with a good attitude when slow play occurs. Or, when the weather gets adverse, one strategy would be to always enjoy the challenge.

But you must do more than just have a plan; implementation is essential. Just ask Kevin Sutherland, winner of the 2002 Accenture World Match Play Championships. During this tournament, the commentators spoke via telephone to Sutherland's brother David, who mentioned how he once turned down Kevin's invitation for a practice round because it was pouring rain. Kevin played and plugged on in the adverse conditions, ultimately preparing himself to hold a trophy in the winner's circle.

Make Every Course Your Favorite

"I love Merion and I don't even know her last name." [26]

—Lee Trevino

There's an old saying in golf: "Different horses for different courses." Some golfers just play better on certain courses. Ben Hogan played so well at both L.A.'s Riviera Country Club and Colonial Country Club in Fort Worth that both were nicknamed "Hogan's Alley." Pebble Beach holds the same magic for Mark O'Meara, who won a U.S. Amateur and several tour events there.

Many factors influence why a particular course provides a comfort zone for a particular player. One is that the course fits the player's eye—the holes just seem to line up well. The course might be a predominately left-to-right-shot course, favoring the right-hander who likes to fade the ball. The premise of course favoritism might be this simple: Players just like some courses more than others, and they talk themselves into playing better on their favorite courses: Jack Nicklaus consistently mentions his love for Augusta National.

On the flip side, consider Lee Trevino, who's won every major except the Masters. Trevino has stated that Augusta National and he were never a good fit.[27] If he felt the love for the Masters that Jack Nicklaus does, he might have won there.

It really is that simple. You can convince yourself that you do not like a certain course, that it does not fit your game. Or you can tell yourself how much you like a course with its great layout and perfect greens. In that case, you will enjoy the course even more because you played so well.

Take It Slow

"You're only here for a short visit, so don't hurry, don't worry, and be sure to stop and smell the flowers along the way." [28]

—Walter Hagen

G ary Player has developed a unique mental strategy to play his best under pressure. [29] He does everything at a slower pace before a tournament. Player removes his clubs from his car slower than usual, takes his time tying his golf shoes, and meanders to the first tee.

This slow-mo strategy directly combats why most of us play poorly under pressure. We tend to get anxious in competition, and when we are anxious, we typically speed up. We walk faster, we talk faster, and we think faster. Even our swing rhythm picks up. When we are anxious, our brain releases such hormones as epinephrine and norepinephrine, which stimulate our blood flow and heart rate, and cause countless other changes throughout our body.

Welcome to the first-tee jitters: Allow "the Gary Player Principle" to help you combat this common golf difficulty. When you arrive at the golf course, take your clubs out of your car very slowly, walk gingerly over to the practice tee, take some slow practice swings, and warm up at a very deliberate pace. When you are ready to hit your first tee shot, think about doing everything a little slower.

Under pressure you will also have a tendency to walk quicker to your ball. Instead, slow down and enjoy the walk. Walking faster increases the heart rate, which in turn can disrupt the rhythm of your golf swing. Take the time to think about the shot that you are about to execute. Once you make your decision, take your club out of the bag a little more slowly, take some practice swings at a gentle pace, and then step up and hit your shot in a nonhurried manner. Slow down, and watch your scores go down.

23

Enjoy, Enjoy, Enjoy

"Toil is the sire of fame. And joy is toil's perfect mate."[30]
—Tom Seaver

Baseball Hall of Famer Willie Stargell once remarked how umpires started the game by shouting "Play ball!" not "Work ball!" Stargell realized his level of play would be much higher if he enjoyed what he was doing. Likewise, Dusty Baker, a former player, said he could recall all the great times he had as a kid playing ball in his backyard, and he would bring those pleasant thoughts to the plate with him.[31]

This philosophy holds true for golf. If you want to play your best, have fun doing it. Fun and anxiety do not mix. They are like oil and water. Your pleasure in the play will purge the nervousness.

In describing the competitive pressure of majors, Jack Nicklaus has used the words "relish" and "pleasure."[32] His ability to enjoy tournament play has helped him compete under the pressure cooker of major championships. Dave Stockton mentioned that his victory at the 1996 Senior U.S. Open was a direct result of his ability to enjoy his experience. His goal that week was to thoroughly enjoy every moment of the tournament, from meeting the tournament volunteers to playing under the competitive gun.

Most amateurs forget to enjoy the day. They get so wrapped up in shooting a good score that they can't have fun if playing poorly or not shooting their handicap. Remember, handicaps are based on your best ten out of twenty rounds. If golfers can only have fun shooting their handicap, then they will find enjoyment only half the time.

You may not always play your best, but you can always commit to having fun. Davis Love Jr. stated it best when he gave his son this timeless bit of wisdom: "Follow your dream and enjoy the trip."[33]

Confidence Is a Choice

"I wonder who's going to finish second." [34]

> —**Tommy Bolt,** after birdieing the first
> hole in the first round en route to his
> victory at the 1958 U.S. Open

While confidence is an essential ingredient for successful golf, it is as fickle as an eight-year-old boy in a candy store. One moment he wants to try the sweet Gummy Bears and the next he will gobble up the sour chews. Good shots on the golf course create the sweet air of invincibility. A couple of bad shots can sour your attitude and perception of your golf ability.

Once we begin to lose our confidence, it is difficult to gain that sweet feeling back again. After a couple of bad shots, it seems as if the game has become our enemy. All we think about is how we are going to miss the next shot. All we seem to be able to do is berate ourselves with negative comments about our lack of ability. Our focus is on the hazards and trouble rather than at the desired fairway or green.

One of the toughest mental skills to acquire is remaining confident when your game takes the train south for the day. However, no matter how poorly you are playing, you can always choose to remain confident. Tom Watson chose to be confident over every putt in the 1982 U.S. Open. Most remember his remarkable chip-in on the seventeenth hole, but more important to his victory was his thought process on the greens. On the seventh hole, he missed a two-foot putt. It didn't even touch the cup. Watson didn't lose confidence in his putting, though; he merely told himself that even great putters miss an occasional easy one.[35]

Confidence is a choice. Winners like Tom Watson choose to remain confident regardless of the situation or past disasters.

Centuries ago the renowned philosopher Rene Descartes wrote that we have the capacity to think whatever we choose.[36] He added that we have the capacity to possess self-liberating thoughts or self-defeating thoughts. More recently, Victor Frankl wrote in his book *Man's Search for Meaning*, "Every human has the freedom to change at any instant. The last of the human freedoms is to choose one's attitude in any given set of circumstances." You have the choice of having a good or bad attitude and the freedom to change your attitude. If you make the correct choice, then the chances are much greater that you will become a better player and the player you want to be.

Find Your Emotional Intelligence for Smarter Golf

"Out-of-control emotions can make smart people stupid." [37]
—**Byron Nelson**

Arnold Palmer once remarked "What separates the great players from the good ones is not so much ability as brain power and emotional equilibrium."[38]

This key to success was identified as far back as ancient Greece. Plato used the term "sophrosyne" to describe the ability to value fortune and disaster in the same light. The Greek philosophers cherished a tempered balance, and they believed qualities such as self-mastery and self-control would transcend time as essentials for a prosperous life.

In today's literature, Daniel Goleman has popularized this same notion in his book *Emotional Intelligence*. Goleman substantiates Arnold Palmer's claim that expertise is not the main predictor of achievement. Rather, it is an awareness of emotions and the ability to manage those emotions effectively.

Emotional intelligence is an essential ingredient in playing smart and successful golf. Scientists have indicated that emotions are the primitive part of the brain and are a carryover from our prehistoric years.[39] Getting angry quickly and losing our temper helped us to stay alive in a hostile world. However, for most of us to stay alive in golf, we must control the primitive emotional part of the brain.

Golf is an exceptionally demanding sport requiring the utmost precision. To be precise on the golf course, you must remain cool, calm, and collected. Drastic emotional swings can negatively affect our concentration and our ability to remain rational in the heat of competition. Bobby Jones was a notorious hothead when he was younger, and he believed his ability began to shine when he learned to control his emotions and remain on an even keel throughout his round.[40]

Some of today's greatest players, however, wear their emotions on their sleeves. Dottie Pepper and Sergio Garcia come to mind. They have the incredible capacity to get extremely emotional and then are able to refocus very quickly and find their balance before the next shot.

While that approach works for those exceptional players, a better fit for the average golfer, and a way to develop a "sophrosyne-type" attitude, is to visualize the wearing of an emotional suit of armor. Every shot, whether good or bad, bounces off this suit, not allowing your attitude to be swayed by the recent events. This armor is a mental mechanism allowing you to ignore any happenings that may cause excessive emotions. Wearing this emotional suit of armor will thicken your skin and will help you become more mentally tough under pressure.

31

14

The Secret Is in the Dirt

"How do you get to Carnegie Hall? Practice, Practice, Practice."
—**Anonymous**

One time after both Gary Player and Ben Hogan had shot a 75 in a U.S. Open, Hogan said to Player, "You're going to be a great player. How much do you practice?" Player proceeded to explain how he practices, and for how long. Hogan then stated, "Double it!"[41]

Hogan was notorious for beating balls before it was "fashionable." That's because he believed that the secret to golf is in the dirt.[42] Hogan said there were not enough hours in the day to practice everything needed to become a great player.

Golf doesn't come easy to anyone. Not to you, not to me, not to Ben Hogan. It might appear easy on television, although we never see all the thousands of hours professional golfers spend off screen hitting practice balls. Nick Faldo estimated that he has hit more than a million practice shots in his life.

Next time you are not playing as well as you'd like, ask yourself how much you practiced this month. Then tell yourself to "Double it." Hogan would be proud of you.

Let Go of the
Perfection Syndrome

"Perfection belongs to the gods; the most that we can hope for is excellence."
—Carl Jung

When Bobby Clampett joined the PGA Tour, he was touted as the game's next great player. His own golf coach at BYU, Karl Tucker, described Clampett as one of the best players he had ever coached. When Clampett needed a 65, Tucker said, he would shoot 65.

Clampett acquired some of his swing knowledge from Homer Kelly's *The Golfing Machine*, which is based on high-order physics and geometry, and breaks down the golf swing into twenty-four main components. The book's subtitle is

"The Computer Age Approach to Golfing Perfection." And that is what Clampett wanted to achieve with his swing.[43]

In one famous instance, Clampett opened with rounds of 66 and 67 at the 1982 British Open, and he held a seven-stroke lead with thirty-one holes to play. Then his game began to unravel. He stumbled to a 78 and 77 on the weekend, finishing tenth. When asked to explain his collapse, he mentioned that he believed his swing was not mechanically sound.[44]

If you become too much of a perfectionist, you begin to convince yourself that you will not hit the ball well or play well unless your swing is perfect. Jack Nicklaus, a winner of eighteen major championships, has commented that he has never played perfect golf in a major. He believes it is unrealistic to think that you need to play perfect golf to win. The key to winning, according to Nicklaus, is getting the ball into the hole, and it really does not matter how.[45]

Champions play the golf course. Their focus is on getting the ball into the cup, not perfection with the golf swing. Take Lee Trevino. Comparing his looping swing on video to what is now considered the "ideal modern" swing, you might think he would have a tough time breaking par. Ditto for Jim Furyk. Ed Furgol was another champion golfer whose swing was far from perfect. Due to a childhood accident in which he broke his left arm, he was incapable of straightening it while playing. Because of his limited flexibility, Furgol created a dipping swing that was self-described as a "whiplike stroke." Through determination and countless hours of practice, Furgol won the 1954 U.S. Open.

Let go of the quest for the perfect swing and find one that works for you.

16

Leak Out Praise

"Sport does not build character: Sport reveals character."
—John Wooden

W*hy do I hit the ball so well on the range, but play so poorly on the golf course?* That's a question that has haunted golfers for ages.

In searching for an answer, let's turn to the psychological principle of Drive Theory, which states that our tendencies are exposed when we are under pressure.[46] Unfortunately, most beginning golfers' swing habits are incorrect. As most golf instruction books will state, the correct golf swing starts from the ground up, with the lower body initiating the sequence of the downswing. Beginning golfers, instead, have a tendency to start the downswing with their shoulders or hands. This can lead to a wide variety of problems such as a loss of power or the dreaded slice.

On the practice range, most amateurs aren't under pressure and can execute their swings more properly. But when they put pressure on their swing by going to the golf course, their bad tendencies get exposed.

Picture a leaky pipe. If it has small cracks in its fundamentals, water should still flow freely without any pressure. Once pressure is put on the pipe with a large amount of water flow, the pipe will start to leak everywhere. That is why beginning golfers see their swing leaking all over the place when they go to the golf course. The cracks in their swing mechanics will show themselves under pressure.

Drive Theory also applies to the mental side of golf. Mental flaws will be exposed under pressure, ranging from lost confidence to a wandering mind to a bad case of nerves. For instance, a golfer with a tendency to become negative will, at the first sign of adverse conditions, begin to lose that loving feeling and start throwing disparaging remarks at everything imaginable. In essence, this golfer has sprouted a serious mental leak.

The secret to plugging those leaks that erupt on the golf course is to possess fundamentally sound physical and mental habits. To acquire appropriate physical mechanics, read instructional books, study instructional tapes, pound range balls, and get some lessons. To possess solid mental mechanics, practice thinking patterns that promote your best golf. One example is making positive self-statements routinely throughout your round. Use this positive approach in all situations, from when you are just playing with your friends on a Saturday afternoon to when you are playing in the club championship. By applying this approach, you will leak out praise for yourself when you are in pressure-packed situations.

The Eyes Have It

"No man sees far: Most see no farther than their noses."
—**Thomas Carlyle**

How many times have you rehashed your round and counted all the putts you should have made? You would easily reduce the score of your round by four or five strokes every time.

The key to great putting is your ability to see the target line, and the key to seeing the target line is where you position your eyes during the setup. Some of the best putters on tour, such as Ben Crenshaw, Phil Mickelson, and Justin Leonard, don't place their eyes directly over the ball. Rather, they position their eyes approximately halfway between the ball and their feet in an eye position called "inside the line."

Placing the eyes directly over the ball is not for everyone. Some individuals may putt more effectively if they place their eyes inside the line like Crenshaw, Mickelson, and Leonard. The important question is, "How do you know which is best for you?"

A University of Florida study found that eye dominance plays a significant role as to where golfers should position their eyes when putting.[47] Just like being right-handed or left-handed, people are left-eye dominant or right-eye dominant. This study found that golfers who had a left dominant eye and were right-handed had a tendency to putt better when their eyes were placed over the ball. Conversely, golfers who were right-eye dominant and right-handed putted better when they positioned their eyes inside the line. The researchers suggested that the bridge of the nose partially blocks the perception of the target line for right-eyed and right-handed golfers when they position their eyes directly over the ball. However, for right-eye and right-handed golfers, the perception of the target line is not obstructed when the eyes are positioned inside the line. The same principle would apply to golfers who are left-eye dominant and left-handed.

It's easy to assess your eye dominance. First, with palms facing away from you, overlap your fingers and thumb of your right hand with the fingers and thumb of your left hand. Next, spread your hands a little apart to create a space between your hands that forms an equilateral triangle with approximately one-inch sides. Then with outstretched arms, scope a target approximately twenty feet away through the space in your hands with both eyes open. The target must be small enough to fit into that space. Close your right eye. If the target is gone, you are right-eye dominant. If the target disappears when you close your left eye, you are left-eye dominant.

If you are right-eye dominant and right-handed, you might benefit from positioning your eyes inside the line, just like Mickelson, Crenshaw, and Leonard do. The secret is to find out where to place your eyes so that you can see the target line with the greatest precision.

18

Be Trigger Happy

"A powerful agent is the right word. Whenever we come upon one of those intensely right words, the resulting effect is physical as well as spiritual." [48]

—Mark Twain

I n the movie *For the Love of the Game*, Kevin Costner portrays a major league pitcher. In one scene, he is pitching against the Yankees at New York. You hear the Yankee fans heckling Costner's character. However, Costner's character has developed a mental strategy to counteract all those distractions. At the start of each of his routines, he says to himself, "Release the mechanism." As soon as he states those magical words, all the fans fall completely silent. More amazing, all he can see is the catcher, batter, and umpire placed within a type of tunnel.

While such a scene seems Hollywood, the mind *can* be trained to enter a higher level of concentration. In his book

Mind over Golf, Dr. Richard Coop recommends some type of behavior to help a player enter into a deeper level, such as pulling the Velcro of the glove on and off. For Tiger Woods, successive eye blinks comprise his trigger for entering into a higher level of focus.[49]

Training your mind to enter a higher level of consciousness can be accomplished in a few steps. First, develop a concentration phrase that consists of a couple of words, such as "complete focus" or "be in the moment," or use the Costner phrase. Next, find a quiet place to sit and relax. Then, visualize yourself stating this concentration phrase at the start of your pre-shot routine. As you state your concentration phase, visualize that everything on the course is blocked out of awareness, except your target. Last, when you are on the course, use the concentration phrase at the start of your routine. In time and with a lot of practice, you will begin to develop a supreme level of Tiger concentration.

19

Have Selective Amnesia
Instead of Rapid Recall

"I've never missed a putt in my mind." [50]

—**Jack Nicklaus**

L ee Trevino once said, "The hardest shot in golf is the one right after a shank." In all his wit and wisdom, Trevino stated a great psychological premise: Past failures create negative images and those negative images hurt our future performance.

Great players usually are ones who can more quickly forget their mistakes. In his book *Putting Out of Your Mind*, Bob Rotella discusses how great players have selective amnesia. Rotella describes how Jack Nicklaus has stated that he has never three-putted the last hole of a tournament. Even when a friend pointed out that he *had* three-putted, Nicklaus insisted he could not remember the event.

Instead of selective amnesia, most amateur golfers have rapid recall. They don't remember the first four holes in which they made all their three-footers, but yet they will quickly recall that missed three-footer on the previous hole. Same goes for that smother hook gone O.B. after four straight drives in the fairway. Rapid recall of this negative baggage hurts our chances of making a good putting stroke or executing an effective swing.

We are told that forgetfulness is a bad trait. That's true when it comes to forgetting where you last put your keys or your wallet. However, forgetfulness can be a desired quality on the golf course, especially when it concerns your history of bad shots.

20

See Negative, Get Negative.
See Positive, Get Positive.

"The mind is its own place and in itself can make a heaven of hell, and a hell of heaven." [51]

—John Milton

Our perception controls our reality. If you have a negative framework, all you can see is negative in your surroundings and your world. If you have a positive framework, you perceive the world as a great and wonderful place. In his book *In Search of Excellence*, Terry Orlick tells a cute story that describes the difference between a negative and positive life framework. [52] A three-year-old girl was riding in a car with her mother and asked, "Where are all the jerks and losers today?" To which the mother responds, "They are only on the road when your dad is driving."

If a golfer possesses a negative framework, then negativity on the course is all that is seen. If a golfer perceives all other tournament participants as having more talent, then intimidation is felt. If the focus is upon all the trouble on a hole, then anxiety levels will rise.

A negative attitude can even spoil a career. Harry Cooper was an extremely talented golfer in the pre-World War II era who won many tournaments. Paul Runyan, one of Cooper's contemporaries, once said that Cooper was one of the best shotmakers of his day, but that he was also one of the most negative persons on tour.[53] To this day, Cooper remains the winningest American male golfer never to have won a major championship.

On the other hand, a golfer with a positive perspective should entice positive events. A golfer who sees only the flagstick rather than all the trouble that lurks on the hole will be more relaxed and thus optimize his performance. Playing with terrible and disruptive partners is seen as an opportunity to work on blocking out outside distractions.

Having a positive perspective even about the weather can also make you achieve great things when Mother Nature isn't on your side. Consider Tom Watson. He grew up in Kansas City where it can be bitterly cold in the winter. Watson knows that when the weather gets bad, he has an advantage. At no time was this more evident than at the 1979 Memorial Tournament. With winds blowing at thirty miles an hour and the wind chill at fifteen below zero, Watson shot a 69 on a day when the scoring average was around 79. Watson said it was one of his most gratifying and enjoyable rounds ever.[54]

Norwegians live in a locale that is often bitter cold, yet they are a nation of outdoor enthusiasts. They have a saying that "There is no such thing as bad weather, only bad clothing."[55] If you believe there are only good days on the golf course, then you are bound to always have a great round, regardless of your score.

21

Harness the Energy of Anxiety

"Having nerves and feeling the pressure just gets you focused and gets your concentration level where it needs to be. I harness that nervous energy into a positive way." [56]

—Tom Lehman

An old adage in sport psychology says, "It's okay to have butterflies. Just make sure you get them to fly in formation." Being anxious isn't necessarily bad and actually has the potential to increase our capability to accomplish extraordinary feats. When we are anxious, our body surges with hormones that promote the accuracy of our eyesight, increase the acuteness of our hearing, and can even enhance the precision of our touch and feel.

Most successful golf professionals know that anxiety is an important part of competitive golf. It can motivate a golfer to demonstrate excellence on the course. Tom Kite, for instance, has stated, "Anxiety is a very positive event; it allows you to do great things."[57] Kite believes that this energy source can help sharpen your senses and make you play at a much greater level than when the event is unimportant and the nerves nonexistent.

Unfortunately, most amateur golfers view anxiety as a negative emotion. They interpret the butterflies and heart palpitations as symptoms indicative of an impending disaster, like the iceberg that sank the *Titanic*. They let their nerves get the best of them, and their game sinks under the pressure.

H. A. Dorfman, a sport psychologist for many professional baseball players, ingeniously illustrates how anxiety can be used as a benefit or as a deficit to performance. Dorfman describes anxiety like a fire in your house. If anxiety is controlled and seen as a positive, it can heat your house. However, when anxiety is uncontrolled and seen as a negative, it can burn your house down.[58] Use anxiety to your advantage. Let it spark you to do great things under pressure.

22

Denial Can Be Your Friend

"Deny your weaknesses so you can take advantage of your strengths."
—**B. J. Harrington**

In the play *Julius Caesar*, William Shakespeare composed the famous line "The fault, dear Brutus, lies not in the stars, but in ourselves." Shakespeare was expounding the eternal wisdom of taking responsibility for our actions. While that is appropriate in many endeavors, taking responsibility for our actions may not always be the best mental strategy for golf.

Why does Arnold Palmer have so many putters, and why does he switch one for another when he is putting poorly? Or why did Jack Nicklaus have a tendency to blame his regular caddie when he hit a bad shot?[59] Two-time Masters champion

52

Denial Can Be Your Friend

Bernhard Langer has been known to blame his clubs rather than himself when he hits a bad shot. These great players have learned that denial can be your friend if used appropriately.

Using denial as a tool for maintaining your confidence is based on attribution theory, which suggests that golfers who blame failure on factors that will change from hole to hole, such as a bad suggestion by the caddy, should remain confident. Next time, the caddy should make a better call and, with it, a more positive result ensues. In his prime, Seve Ballesteros was never likely to take the blame when he missed putts. If he missed, *something* must have caused the ball from finding the bottom—a spike mark or a noisy camera. Given that those factors should not occur on the next hole, denial allowed Ballesteros to trust his stroke throughout the round.[60]

On the other hand, golfers who blame failure on a lack of ability lose confidence very quickly when things go awry: Skill level doesn't readily change from hole to hole. Thus, if a golfer blames a flawed putting stroke for a string of misses, then a loss of confidence in the player's putting stroke will most likely occur in subsequent holes. Once that happens, it's an uphill battle to regain confidence.

This mental strategy must be qualified. Great golfers are great self-regulators, and they can fix a problem very quickly. However, there are many times when there are no clear answers as to why putts are being missed or why the shot was hit so poorly. In these instances, let denial be your friend. Second, deny during the round, but after the round go to the putting green or range and try to solve the problem. Only use denial during the heat of a round in order to maintain your confidence. After the round, take Shakespeare's advice and shoulder responsibility for your actions and fix your problem.

Be Like Mike

"Golf is a percentage game, and I play the percentages."
—**Byron Nelson**

Michael Jordan has many exceptional traits: great basketball player, great pitchman, great team leader. One trait of his that most people don't know is that MJ is also a basketball statistician. He knows that basketball percentages are tallied by misses and makes, and that misses and makes come in clusters.

Say Jordan averages 50 percent shooting from the field. That doesn't necessarily mean he'll hit five shots in a row and then miss five. Rather, one sequence could be two misses in a row followed by four hits followed by three misses followed by four hits followed by three misses. The sequence can have many different variations. But at the end of the season when you add up the hits and misses, you will get five buckets for every ten shots attempted.

One of Jordan's greatest weapons is that he doesn't let his misses affect his confidence level. He knows that he will at certain times during a game miss consecutive shots. However, he keeps on shooting because he knows that he will eventually get on a hot streak again.

Statistics in golf play out the same way. Let's say you average 2.0 putts on the green per round. In this case, you are bound to have a couple of three-putts in a row, a lot of two-putts, and some one-putts.

As in Charles Dickens's memorable words, "It was the best of times, it was the worst of times," golf parallels our life cycles with its many peaks and valleys. During the worst of times, you need to be a golf statistician. Don't let a sequence of three-putt greens get you down. Play the percentages. Remain confident, and know that the best of times are yet to come.

Find Your Dream, Develop a Plan, Pay the Price

"Our future will be determined in large part by our dreams and by the struggle to make them real." [61]

—**Mihaly Csikszentmihaly**

Greg Norman had a dream. He believed that by the time he was thirty, he would be the best player in the world, married to an American, and a millionaire. His vision directed all his focus and energies toward his goals. By the time he was thirty, Norman had achieved his dream. [62]

Dreams are essential to success, but they are not enough. You must also devise a plan. Say you are a college player and your dream is to make the PGA Tour. However, you believe your ability to concentrate is a big hindrance to achieving this ultimate goal. You will need a goal-setting plan to improve your concentration level.

The first step is to evaluate your current level of concentration during a round. Construct a rating scale of one to ten, with ten being your highest level. Recall a day when your concentration level was at its peak and give that a ten. Next, recall a day of your absolute worst focus and give that a one. Then describe each of the other eight levels on the scale. With scale in hand, start rating your levels of concentration during rounds. Rate each hole of the round to discover any trends. Do this for at least five rounds.

Your next step is to set short-term goals. Let's say you found that your average level of concentration during a round is six. However, you also discovered that your concentration waned at the end of the round to an average of three. Based on this evaluation, you could have two short-term goals: (1) Increase your overall concentration to a seven for the next five rounds; (2) Increase your concentration level for holes fifteen through eighteen to a four. Set goals that increase by 20 percent each month, thus keeping your goals challenging yet attainable.

Next, devise strategies to help you accomplish those goals. To increase your overall level of focus, develop a pre-shot routine. According to Bob Rotella, a routine is one of the best methods to instill concentration.[63] To increase your concentration level at the end of the round, your strategy could entail getting in better shape. Once we are fatigued, our concentration diminishes. Getting in better shape should help a golfer remain focused throughout the round.

The last step in your plan is to evaluate your improvement each week. If your concentration is getting better, stick with it. However, if your focus is not improving, then you need to change your strategy. Perhaps your pre-shot routine is not as effective as it should be. You may need to incorporate some visualization and self-talk into your routine. The key is to find a strategy that keeps you improving.

Texas oil billionaire Bunker Hunt was asked how to succeed. He said, "Find your dream, devise a plan, and then pay the price."[64] While devising and implementing a plan takes a lot of energy, the attainment of your dream is worth it.

Risk the Pain of Losing

"It is only by risking our persons from one hour to another that we live at all."

—**William James**

Most athletes will say that the most dangerous opponent is one who is sick or injured. Such an opponent is in a no-lose situation. If they lose, they have an excuse. If they win, it shows how talented they are. The injury or sickness is a handicap that protects the ego. When there's no cost to your ego, there's no holding back and you're a danger to everyone.

Psychologists have labeled this handicapping phenomenon the Deschappelles Coup, named for the nineteenth-century French chess champion Alexandre Deschapelles.[65] He was a world-class player with great insecurities about his abilities. He would only play an opponent if that person would remove one of Deschapelles's pawns and then make the first move. Thus, he would not look like a fool if he lost. His coup supported his fragile ego.

You have probably met golfers who use the Deschappeles Coup. When a big tournament is approaching, they have a tendency to practice very little or none at all. Then, if they play poorly, they can blame it on their limited practice time and hectic schedule. But if they play well, they look that much better given their limited playing time.

Another type of self-handicapping is to quit or give up in a competition. Giving up protects the ego because the person doesn't risk all he has in order to win or play well. Athletes from all sports have said that the pain of losing is much greater than the thrill of victory. Quitting buffers that pain.

Hale Irwin described playing golf in competition akin to standing naked in front of a big crowd where everyone can see all your faults.[66] Some golfers will try to cover up, by self-handicapping. However, golfers who are willing to lay all their golf nakedness on the line are the ones who are more likely to achieve their potential.

Serenity Now

"Give me the strength to accept the things I cannot control,
the courage to change the things I can control,
and the wisdom to know the difference between the two."
— **Reinhold Niebuhr,** in the Serenity Prayer

In his autobiography *Golf My Way*, Jack Nicklaus urges top professionals and amateurs alike to focus only on factors within their control. Nicklaus states that the only thing a player can control is his own game and further adds that being concerned about factors outside his control is not only a distraction, but a waste of energy. Annika Sorenstam states that once the ball leaves her clubface, she ceases to worry about it. This philosophy has allowed her to accept any outcome that occurs on the course.[67]

Serenity Now

Here is a mental exercise for golf based on the Serenity Prayer used by many sport psychologists. List all the worries you have on the golf course. Next, place the worries in two categorical boxes: "factors I can control" and "factors I cannot control." With the worries you placed into the "cannot control" box, be like Sorenstam, and find the mental strength to accept those factors over which you have no control. Let them go. A helpful mental exercise is to visualize placing the worries into a balloon and letting them float away.

Now here comes the courage part. With the worries you placed into your "control box," devise one strategy for each of those worries. This will help reduce the anxiety associated with each distracting thought. If you worry about the wind, have a strategy to practice low-trajectory shots. After you have developed strategies to eliminate those worries, you will then need to find the courage to practice them.

When you learn to let go of the things you cannot control and focus only on factors within your control, you will discover your serenity on the golf course.

Let Go of Results

"I think golfers get over concerned with results. Enjoy the process: enjoy the opportunity to play." [68]

—**Wendy Ward,** LPGA golfer

Former football coaching great Jimmy Johnson once told his players about the downfalls of focusing on the outcome of the event. Johnson referenced the construction worker who must focus on one step at a time when crossing a beam a thousand feet in the air. If the construction worker looked down and thought about how high he was (the outcome), he would get extremely nervous and be more inclined to fall. However, by focusing on placing one foot in front of the other, the worker wouldn't get as nervous and could easily traverse the beam.

Let Go of Results

The same principle goes for the golf course. Looking down at your scorecard can contribute to higher levels of anxiety, leading to a fall into a poorly played round.

To play their best, golfers must disregard outcome thinking. Brad Faxon, one of the game's best putters, says that when he is putting his best, he doesn't care if he makes the putt. He views making and missing the putt as equals.[69]

When elite golfers recall a zone experience, they also mention that they are not aware of outcomes or scores. Al Geiberger mentioned that he had this type of mental approach when he gave his virtuoso performance at the Memphis Open, becoming the first tour player to shoot 59 in a tour-sanctioned event. When recalling this event, Geiberger stated that he was not aware of his score or whether he was about to break 60 for the first time until the very end of his round.[70]

The opposite of the zone is a slump, and letting go of results might also help end the slump. Corey Pavin mentioned that he entered a severe slump at the end of the 1980s when he started focusing on shooting low scores instead of playing the needed shot. When he got back to just playing golf and creating shots, his slumping pattern began to recede.[71]

A great strategy that can help you let go of results-oriented thinking is to play a round of golf without keeping score. Your task is to think only about the shot at hand, not to be concerned with how many over or under par you are at any time during the round. At the completion of the round, you would then recall each hole and add up your score. Or, better yet, play with a friend who keeps your score.

Once you learn to let go of results-oriented thinking, you begin to get a grip on your best golf.

Go West

"All other things being equal, greens break to the West."[72]
—Harvey Penick

More than a hundred years ago, Horace Greeley told us to go West to find our fame and fortune. The same goes for golf: Not to *go* West, but to focus *on* the West. Most putts are influenced by the grain, and the grain is influenced by how the grass grows. Most grasses grow toward the setting sun. So, if you know which direction is west, you may make a better decision about how much or how little the ball will break.

Grain is influenced by many other factors, too. Sometimes grain grows toward a particular valley. Grain will also lean toward a big body of water or grow toward a mountain range. Grain, as they say, is very fickle.

All great putters are grain aficionados: They know that grain will greatly influence the roll of the ball. It can make your putt break uphill or make it break twice as hard downhill.

Accounting for the grain can add up to a lot of putts made. Jack Nicklaus made his incredible Sunday back-nine charge at the 1986 Masters utilizing skill, experience, purpose, and desire. Augusta's seventeenth hole stands out from the others when it came to his experience at reading the greens. Nicklaus had about a ten-footer with a left-to-right break. Son Jackie, Jack's caddy, thought it was a left-edge putt. But Big Jack knew that Rae's Creek would influence the putt, making the ball break more right than it appeared. Nicklaus decided to play the ball a little more left of the hole and rolled the ball into the cup.[73] The rest is history.

Next time you are deciphering the roll of the putt, do not just use the slope of the green. Be sure to incorporate the grain into your read, and you should find your fame and fortune on the greens.

Are You a Hogan or a Trevino?

"The more I focus, the less I worry about pressure." [74]

—**Nick Price**

Some competitive players believe that acting like Ben Hogan will help them play their best under pressure. Hogan was aloof and steely-eyed in tournaments, not noticing anyone in the gallery or even his playing partners' shots. One time when Hogan and Claude Harmon were paired for a practice round at the Masters, Harmon aced the twelfth, which Hogan birdied. Walking to the thirteenth tee, Hogan was so preoccupied with his own play that he had to ask Harmon what he had just gotten back on the twelfth.

Hogan said his stoic demeanor was the only way he could focus totally on what he was doing. It also buffered him from the stress and anxiety of tournament golf. Other players follow this same philosophy. Nick Faldo comes to mind. So does David Duval, who puts on those wraparound shades and becomes a man of steel, rarely cracking a smile or speaking during his round.

There is more than one way to deal with tournament stress. Look at Lee Trevino. He is a chatterer, continually talking to his playing partners, his caddy, or the gallery. Trevino's jovial attitude helps him combat his nerves. One time in a major, Trevino's playing partner admitted that he was nervous and didn't feel like talking. Said Trevino, "That's okay. I'll do enough talking for the both of us."[75]

If you tried the Hoganesque attitude and feel drained and burned out following a round of golf, then perhaps this isn't the best way for you to deal with competitive anxiety. You might want to try the Trevino method with lots of laughs and chatter. The key is to find which method works best for you and to conduct yourself accordingly.

30

Avoid a Good Walk Spoiled

"If you can't enjoy the time between the golf shots, then you are going to have a pretty difficult life because most of your life is the time spent in-between."[76]
—**Peter Jacobsen**

Jim Loehr, a sport psychologist to some of the greatest tennis players, discovered that the time between points is the most crucial to tennis success. Tennis players with a consistent routine typically played their best under pressure, whereas tennis players who varied their routine were more likely to choke under pressure. According to Loehr, a consistent routine lowers the heart rate down to appropriate levels. A varied routine produces higher heart rates, which can contribute to diminished performance.

Golfers, unlike tennis players, typically don't have to get their heart rates down quickly between shots. However, a poor shot can induce anger and an accompanying jump in heart rate. The result is a good walk to the ball spoiled. More important, that rage can lead to a lack of concentration on the next shot and a compensation for the last poor shot that makes matters even worse.

To prevent this downward spiral, a golfer should employ a post-shot routine. Most golf psychology books will tout a pre-shot routine for best performance, although what you do *after* a shot can also greatly influence your golf performance.

While a post-shot routine isn't recommended for every shot, a routine after a poor shot can be beneficial. Try a post-shot routine based on Loehr's system that incorporates the three r's: release, re-imagine, and reset. After a poor shot, the golfer must first release this negative energy. This can be accomplished by taking deep breaths or making a tight fist for three seconds and then opening your fist while visualizing letting go of a negative ball of energy that dissipates into the sky.

After the release stage, the golfer enters the reimagine phase. Take a practice swing and see an image of the desired shot. The key is to feel the correct swing and see a positive image of the preferred ball flight. Maybe it's that flushed five-iron you struck two weeks ago. The key is to move forward with a positive image and feeling.

The last step involves resetting the mind to focus on only the next shot. Using a self-statement such as "this shot" can be very helpful to remind the player of being in the present. When all three stages of the post-shot routine are completed, the golfer is ready for a good walk—unspoiled—to the ball.

Fail Forward

"It is by my sorrows that I can soar."[77]

—Mahatma Ghandi

Before he started winning major tournaments, Nick Faldo was known as Nick Foldo. His swing wouldn't hold up under pressure. Intent on winning majors, Faldo resolved to rebuild his swing and find what would work for him under pressure.[78] Faldo became a winner because he viewed his failures as a vehicle that would transport him to the top echelon of his profession, and he eventually won three Masters and three British Opens.

To achieve your golf potential, think like Faldo. Embrace your mistakes. Learn from them, move on, and fail forward. An ancient Buddhist saying says, "The arrow that hits the bull's eye is the result of a hundred misses." See failure as a great way to progress forward in your golfing skills.

In his book *Failing Forward,* John Maxwell outlines many principles that can apply to golfers experiencing failure on the golf course. First, understand that making mistakes and failing are inevitable in golf as they are in all sports. Consider Jack Nicklaus: Although he won eighteen majors as a professional, there were more than a hundred times he didn't win. Or look at Michael Jordan, who has missed more than nine thousand shots, many of them potential game winners, during his basketball career.

Second, Maxwell says, if you perceive that a failure has occurred, take yourself out of the equation. See that the *event* was a failure, not you. Third, evaluate your mistakes and learn from them. Mahatma Ghandi was exemplary in how he saw his life as a set of experiments, with each experience helping to find his path to self-realization. He would reflect upon each failure, learn from it, share what he learned, and then jump into his next action with even more vigor.[79]

As a method for your self-realization and progression in golf, create a "failing forward" journal. After each round, write down five mistakes you made. Then write down what you may have learned from each mistake, and move on. The importance of this mental exercise is that you no longer dwell on your previous mistakes. Focus only on what you gained in knowledge from each experience.

But don't just *think* about what you should have done; go out and *practice* the skills you need to improve. As legendary basketball coach John Wooden once said, "Failure is not failure unless it is failure to change."[80]

32

Be Your Own Best Friend

*"I know of no more encouraging fact than the unquestionable ability of
man to elevate his life by a conscious endeavor."*
—**Henry David Thoreau**

Billy Mills's is the classic story of Olympic success. A
Native American who grew up on a reservation, he
loved to run and eventually earned a track scholarship to
the University of Kansas, only to drop out and join the service when he found he couldn't perform to his or his coach's
expectations. In the service, however, he felt he could train
without prejudice and focus on his goal of becoming a great
runner.

Mills knew that in order to be the world's best 10,000-
meter runner, he would have to train his mind as well as his

body. Every day he would sit down with his journal and write positive self-statements about the next Olympics. He wrote such affirmations as "You are going to feel great the day of the run," and "You are going to win in Tokyo." Mills believed that the positive self-statements would trigger his body to respond appropriately and achieve great things. It worked, as Mills won the 10,000-meter gold at the 1964 Olympics in Tokyo.[81] His inspirational story was later made into the movie *Running Brave* starring Robbie Benson.

All great champions intuitively are their own best cheerleaders. From a very young age Gary Player grasped the importance of positive thinking. One day a schoolteacher passed a room where Player was talking to himself in the mirror, repeatedly saying, "I'm going to be the greatest player in the game's history." After watching Player repeat this more than fifty times, the teacher gave up counting and left.[82]

Unfortunately, most golfers jump at the chance to degrade their skills. When things turn sour out on the golf course, these players become saturated with negativity. Such a player becomes his own worst enemy, cutting down his own experience and downgrading his own game.

However, to play your best and think like a winner, you must become your best friend on the course. One way to have a winning mentality is to create and develop a "best friend journal." Every day, you write one positive self-statement about your game, physical or mental. One day you might write that you are a great sand player. Another entry would be how much you love competition. Keep this book in your golf bag, and when you have a few moments, read a few entries for a positive mental jolt.

In *How I Play the Game*, Tiger Woods wrote, "Never beat yourself up, because there are plenty of people who will do it for you." Being your own best friend is the first step toward playing your best golf.

Build Confidence
by Association

"Really great people make you feel that you, too, can become great."
—Mark Twain

Not long after Tiger Woods turned professional, tour veteran Mark O'Meara emerged as something akin to a big brother for Woods. O'Meara gave tips to Woods on the many nuances of tour life. Soon they were Florida neighbors and friends, getting together for fun practice rounds whenever they could. Sometimes Woods wins these friendly matches, and sometimes O'Meara prevails.

While Woods has gained a lot from this friendship, so has O'Meara. One major benefit for O'Meara has been a significant boost in confidence. Notice how after Woods won his first major, the Masters, in 1997, O'Meara the very next year won both the Masters and the British Open—after having played the tour for more than fifteen years without a major victory. Chances are that in witnessing Woods's tremendous victory at the 1997 Masters, O'Meara probably consciously or subconsciously said to himself, "Hey, I can beat this guy sometimes at home. And this guy can win the Masters and dominate the tour. Then I must have the ability to win a major." He built his confidence by association.

Confidence by association can work at any level. A very good college golfer once expressed how he had gained confidence from his association with a talented teammate, who was one of the nation's top players. The former beat the latter out of a dollar in a friendly match. He didn't spend the dollar, but rather posted it on his locker to remind him of his victory, which always gave him a jolt of confidence.

What can a dollar buy nowadays? Plenty, if used properly.

Temper Your Competitive Fire with *Self-Mastery*

"My only goal is to look back at the end of each year and see that I have improved." [83]

—Jim Furyk

The American way is to be the best. We are led to believe that being number one is all that matters. While being the best has its many perks, focusing only on that goal can be detrimental to performance as well as mental health.

Not all cultures value being number one. Some Eastern cultures value self-mastery as the mainstay for enlightenment. Consider the parable of the American tourist who found himself in Japan on the day of a pilgrimage to the top of a sacred mountain. The tourist, who had been active all his life and in great shape, decided to join the pilgrimage.

After twenty minutes he was out of breath and could hardly climb another step, while the elderly and the young villagers easily moved past him. "I don't understand it," he said to his Japanese companion. "How can all these villagers easily climb the mountain, yet it is so difficult for me?"

His friend answered, "You have the typical American attitude and you see everything as a competition. You see the mountain as your enemy and you set out to conquer it. So, naturally the mountain fights back and wins. However, our culture does not see the mountain as our enemy, but a friend—a friend that will guide us along the way.[84]

When a golfer believes that his or her only goal is to be the best, the goal is almost always unattainable. Whatever level of play—high school, college, or pros—only a few people can ever be the best. It's like fighting the mountain. Researchers have found that this type of attitude (a competitive orientation) can lead to many complications such as burnout, poor sportsmanship, greater anxiety, less joy in the sport, and lower performance.

By contrast, there are golfers who have a mastery orientation, believing that each level up the mountain is the challenge. The goal is to get better in all skills rather than to be the best. A mastery-oriented golfer is competing against himself. Nick Price exhibits a mastery orientation and has said, "I play and give each shot 100 percent, and I'm not thinking about winning or about what score I'm shooting. I'm just doing my best on every shot."[85] When the focus is on improvement rather than winning, golfers are more likely to enjoy their sport, be less anxious, be less likely to burn out, and perform better.[86]

While it appears that a mastery orientation has benefits, this might not be the best strategy for achieving at the highest level. It is the competition that creates the fire that burns bright in many golfers, and this competitive fire propels them to practice all those long hours. Perhaps the key to reaching the mountaintop is to have a balance between mastery and competitive orientations. Ben Hogan is a great example: He mentioned that he loved to win, but he also relished improvement in his shotmaking skills.[87] To find your excellence, value winning but also continually strive for improvement.

Finding the Zone

"We are what we repeatedly do. Excellence, then, is not an act, but a habit."
—Aristotle

Most of us call it "the zone," that magical yet elusive place where we can do no wrong on the golf course. Every putt seems to drop, and every drive finds the middle of the fairway. It is a time when this difficult game seems so easy.

Psychologist Mihaly Csikszentmihaly has another word for the zone—flow. He has studied the experience of flow in tens of thousands of people around the world ranging from surgeons to business executives to artists to athletes.[88] Dr. "C" found that the flow state of optimal performance occurs when certain components are in place. The first is facing a task that is challenging yet attainable. If the task is too easy, individuals get bored and lose their way. When athletes believe they can meet the demands of the situation, the second component is in place: confidence.

The third component involves having an appropriate intensity level. Athletes describe this as being calm but energized. When an athlete is calm, energized, and confident, then the next component falls into place—an intense focus on the task at hand. They are completely immersed in the task and the outside world does not exist. The last component is enjoying the situation. Observe any athlete who's in flow, and you will typically see a big smile.

While research has described these as essential components of flow, this optimal state of performance is unique to each individual. In *The Game I Love*, Sam Snead described the zone as a feeling of being "cool mad." He was relaxed but highly intense about his game. Likewise, David Duval has mentioned that he plays his best when he feels a little irritated.[89] On the other hand, Bobby Locke stated that he played his best when he possessed a calm deportment, something he called "a benign imperturbability."[90]

Given that the flow state is unique, you need to create your own road map to finding your flow state more often. Try using a flow log, an account of your peak performance experiences. Record everything you did prior to a great round, such as how much you slept the night before, what you ate for breakfast, and how much you practiced that week. You also want to record all your thoughts and feelings during the round. Pay attention to detail and describe your level of intensity, what and where you were focusing your attention, and your thoughts concerning your confidence level. Also record the date and golf course you played.

Hopefully, you have a couple of flow experiences to chart. Study them to see if any patterns emerged during your flow experiences. Resolve to repeat those patterns of behavior before an event. Ultimately, your flow log will act as your guide to finding the zone.

36

Let Edison's Optimism Enlighten Your Game

"Optimism is a kind of heart stimulant—the digitalis of failure."
—Elbert Hubbard

Thomas Edison is known as one of the greatest inventors of all time. While many would point to his creative genius for his many inventions, it may have been his attitude about his many failures which proved to be his greatest asset. Edison said that he tried and failed more than a thousand times before succeeding at inventing an effective light bulb. He saw every failure as a temporary roadblock to his future success.

Edison was the epitome of an optimist. Optimists view failure as something that is within their control. They believe that their actions can influence subsequent failures. That is why optimists will continually persist even in the face of many failed attempts.

Pessimists, by contrast, view failure as something outside their control. They take the view that failure is more likely to be around for a long time, believing that their actions won't have a substantial impact on subsequent failures. As a result, they are much more likely to give up when failure is upon them.

Failure is rampant in golf, from experiencing a bad hole or terrible tournament to not advancing in Q-School. Golfers who do not give up after they have failed are much more likely to achieve their dreams. Martin Seligman, author of *Learned Optimism*, states that an optimistic attitude can be acquired with the appropriate thinking patterns. Seligman believes anyone can relearn and change their thought patterns to become more optimistic.

Based on Seligman's work, here are some fundamental rules for becoming more optimistic on the golf course: (1) See failure and setbacks as temporary. Former U.S. Open champion and TV golf analyst Ken Venturi said that the cycle of a golfing life is finding what works, losing it, and then finding it again. See your bad play as part of a downward cycle in the scheme of your golfing life; (2) See your poor play as a problem with your strategy or technique. Perhaps your failure to score is a result of your putting technique. Try the belly putter or left-hand-low style. (3) If you failed recently in a tournament, you should evaluate whether the failure was due to the course not fitting your game. Not every golf course is going to match up well with your style of play. (4) View that your ability level will improve over time. For instance, if you are a freshman in college, realize that your scoring average should improve while you are in school.

Adopt the Edison philosophy, and wait for your excellence to shine.

Keep It Simple,
Hit It Farther

"The simpler I keep things, the better I play." [91]

—Nancy Lopez

The familiar motto "Keep it simple, stupid" applies to many facets of life, including golf.

Butch Harmon, Tiger Woods's longtime teacher, said, "It is much easier to have one swing thought than many." [92] Having fewer swing thoughts will also make you hit the ball farther.

The relationship between the amount of swing thoughts and the distance a golfer can hit the ball is based on Hick's Law, a psychological principle that postulates that your reaction time is relative to the number of decisions you make. Your reaction time will increase by a constant (approximately 120 milliseconds) when your decisions are doubled. If you have one thought, your reaction time will be approximately 190 milliseconds. If you have two thoughts, your reaction time increases to 310 milliseconds. If you have four decisions to make, then your reaction time again increases to 430 milliseconds, etc.[93]

The more swing thoughts you have on the downswing, the slower the brain will send the signal to your muscles. If you have one swing thought, the signal will be sent much faster to your muscles than if you were to have four swing thoughts, and the faster the signal is sent, the faster you can swing the club on the downswing. Most important, the faster you can swing the club, the farther you should be able to hit the ball.

Einstein's philosophy about science and life was to "keep it simple, but do not make it simpler." Golf is a complex game, but we do not have to think about all the complexities while swinging. Keep it simple, hit it farther.

Winners Imitate Winners

"Study the actions of illustrious men to see how they have borne themselves, examine the causes of their victories and defeats, so as to imitate the former and avoid the latter."

—Machiavelli

Trivia question: Who won the 1986 Masters? That's easy—Jack Nicklaus. Now try this one: Who was paired with Nicklaus that Sunday? None other than Sandy Lyle, who would win at Augusta just two years later.

Next: Who won the 1978 Masters? Gary Player did. And who was paired with Player in the last round? Hint: It was a young Spaniard. Seve Ballesteros had the fortune of watching Player birdie seven of the last ten holes in '78 to win. The very next year, Ballesteros won his first major, the British Open, and in 1980 he won his first Masters.

Lyle and Ballesteros both were fortunate enough to watch and learn how two all-time greats handle the intense pressure of the back nine at Augusta National. Something good rubbed off on them.

While most of us will never play the final round of the Masters with the eventual winner, many of us get to compete in tournaments alongside excellent players performing well in crunch time. Or maybe it's the chance to play with your club champion during a Saturday afternoon Nassau. When these opportunities present themselves, observe these experts very closely. Watch their mannerisms and see how your patterns of behavior may be different from theirs. Most likely, you will notice that the highly skilled player remains focused and calm during the intense pressure. They also will keep to their routine regardless of the situation.

But do more than observe. Once you learn some important behaviors, pattern your actions after them. Imitation isn't only the sincerest form of flattery, it can be the ticket to immediate improvement. Just choose your subjects wisely.

Inoculate Yourself
Against Choking

"I try to simulate the most difficult conditions the players will encounter during competition." [94]

—**Mike Holder,** Oklahoma State golf
coach and winner of eight national championships

Everyone chokes at one time or another when they are under pressure. Even the pros. One of the poster boys for the big choke is Jean Van de Velde, who blew a three-shot lead at the last hole of the 1999 British Open and then lost to Paul Lawrie in a three-way play-off.

Sport psychologists are discovering methods to help prevent athletes from choking under competitive pressure. One strategy involves the motor-learning principle of situational similarity: When practice situations simulate pressure conditions, a greater transfer of skills takes place. Sport scientists at Michigan State University validated this point in an experiment featuring three groups of golfers who learned the task of putting. One group learned putting under normal conditions. Group No. 2 had to repeat the word "cognition" as they putted, the idea being to distract the mind from the pressure of making the putt. Group No. 3 learned putting while being videotaped so as to simulate the self-awareness provoked when a golfer plays in competition.

Interestingly, no differences between the groups were reported when they were reassessed under a low-stress condition. However, when the golfers were placed in a competitive-type situation in which they would earn money based on their performance, the third group performed the best. Learning how to putt using the videotape best simulated the intense pressure of competition, helping these individuals transfer their skills most effectively to pressure-packed situations.[95]

One of the best ways to inoculate yourself against choking is by placing pressure on yourself during practice. Ken Green, a top tour player in the late eighties and early nineties, said he would taunt himself in practice by stating out loud that he would stick a five-dollar bill in the cup if he missed a key putt. When he missed, the group behind him was that much richer. Phil Mickelson has been known to stay out on the practice green for hours trying to make a hundred three-footers in a row. If he misses one, he has to start all over.

You can apply the same logic to all aspects of your practice time. For instance, when hitting your driver on the range, do not just pound balls anywhere and everywhere. Practice hitting your balls to an imaginary fairway and see how many you can hit out of ten. Then make the fairway tighter. Better yet, get a friend and place a meager wager on who hits the most fairways out of ten. Using this type of practice mentality will help you transfer your best swings to competition.

Are You a Nick Faldo
or a Fred Couples?

"Be who you really are." [96]

—Sergio Garcia

Nick Faldo and Fred Couples are worlds apart in their mental approach to the game.

Faldo is analytical and tightly wound. In the eighties he and his teaching guru David Leadbetter tore down Faldo's swing piece by piece and then put it back together. Faldo is the type of player who wants to know how each facet of his swing works, often fiddling with his swing between shots, making sure each part of the puzzle fits.

Then there's Couples, whose silky-smooth, almost nonchalant swing matches his laid-back persona. While he works hard at his game, Couples's incredible natural talent has allowed him to become much less analytical about his swing. When discussing his mental approach, Couples has said he tries to not have *any* swing thoughts other than his intended target.[97]

One key to successful golf is to pinpoint which mental approach works best for you. If you are very analytical like Faldo, you will probably favor having at least a few swing thoughts in your routine. Blanking your mind of all thoughts might actually hinder your performance. On the other hand, if your attitude parallels Couples's, your best play will come when your mind is clear and your attention is all-target.

Carl Jung, in considering the many different approaches to a healthy and successful life, once said, "The shoe that fits one person, pinches another."[98] Be who you *really* are. Find a mental approach that best fits your personality.

Laugh Yourself
to Better Scores

"They laugh that wins."

—**Shakespeare** (from *Othello*)

Jimmy Demaret was one of the most colorful and amica-
ble professionals ever to play golf. He also was known for
his quick wit and jovial attitude. He was once known to say,
"The Bible teaches an eye for an eye, a tooth for a tooth. I
think that is a little harsh. I believe in a joke for a joke."[99] But
Demaret had plenty of game to go with the grins. He won
the Masters three times as well as many other tour events,
intimating that his success was probably a combination of a
festive attitude and talent.

Laughter can be one of your best antidotes to a bad
day on the golf course. Researchers have suggested that

laughter releases hormones known as endorphins that are considered the brain's natural opiates, giving you a sense of euphoria. In essence, laughing can make you feel good about your bad scores. A good chuckle can also make you concentrate better. When we laugh, our brain releases hormones that can rouse our level of alertness.[100]

The power of laughter goes far beyond the golf course. In *Anatomy of an Illness*, Norman Cousins described how he recovered from a debilitating illness by watching a variety of comedy shows and laughing himself to better health.

The choice is simple. You can get angry after every bad shot and in life's tough situations. In this case, you will probably ruin your round and your health. Or, you can laugh at all your mistakes on the golf course and in your life. In that case you will play better, enjoy yourself more, and be able to spend many more days on the golf course due to your great health.

Get Rid of the Irony
in Your Game

"Try to think where you want to put the ball, not where you don't want it to go." [101]

—**Billy Casper**

Please don't think of a pink elephant. So, what did you just think about? What else but a pink elephant. Psychologists relate this phenomenon to the ironic-process theory.[102] By telling yourself not to think about something, it will actually force your thoughts in the unwanted direction. Thus the irony.

Sport scientists have also discovered this phenomenon pertains admirably to the athletic domain. For instance, the mere mention of the word *choke* can cause a decrease in performance.[103] Again, the irony is that by telling yourself *not* to choke, you are much more likely *to* choke.

Likewise, athletes who focus on playing not to lose will typically end up losing. A classic case involved tennis superstar Monica Seles in her semifinal Wimbledon singles match in 1990 against Zina Garrison. After the match Seles said, "I was going for the safety shots. I was scared to hit for winners." She was playing not to lose. Garrison, on the other hand, told herself, "None of this tentative stuff. If I miss at least I'll know that this time I went for it." Garrison was playing to win. Game, set, and match for Garrison.[104]

Bobby Jones said one of his greatest weaknesses as a young player was his trying to avoid hazards instead of playing for a desired target. He believed that he would have won a lot more tournaments if he had focused on what he wanted to do instead of what he was trying to avoid.[105]

When you tell yourself not to hit the ball into the water, you focus your attention on the blue stuff. Telling yourself not to hit it out of bounds redirects your mental energies toward those little white stakes. The same goes for the short game. When chipping on a tight lie, a common self-statement is "Don't flub it." Of course, you flub it.

The way to become less ironic on the course is to reframe your thoughts and self-statements toward what you want to accomplish. Instead of saying, "Don't hit it into the water," reframe it in your mind and state, "Hit this down the middle of the fairway." Or instead of saying, "Don't chili-dip this one," you should be thinking only about chipping it close or holing it. Reframing your thinking in a positive way focuses all your energies in the desired direction, resulting in a more positive outcome. How ironic we didn't think of all this before.

43

Map Out Your Excellence

"Even before you step to the ball, have a full battle plan for the hole worked out." [106]

—Arnold Palmer

In 2002 Lance Armstrong won his fourth consecutive Tour de France. Although Armstrong has exceptional cardiovascular capacity, it takes much more than just a strong heart to win this grueling race. Motivation, an incredible training regime, and a precise racing plan fit into his formula. [107]

But he didn't always race with a well-conceived master plan. In his early years of racing, Armstrong believed he consistently attacked with a "go all-out aggressive, in-your-face" attitude. His explosive power and aggressive style worked for him in short events, although he eventually realized it would never work for the long haul of the Tour de France with its two thousand miles spread over twenty-one stages.

Miguel Cervantes once wrote that the man who is prepared has his battle half fought. Armstrong developed a racing plan suitable for Tour de France success by studying the Tour Bible, a guidebook that shows every stage of the course with profiles of the route. Using this guide, he created a plan that allowed him to stay close to the leaders, but which also permitted him to use his explosive power when needed.

Such preparation and planning is also conducive to winning golf tournaments. Champions know when to attack the course and when to pull back on the reins. Ben Hogan was one of the all-time great planners. When he was on the road, he would bring a blackboard with him to his hotel room, where he would map out each hole and then devise a strategy for each.[108] While warming up on the range before a tournament round, Hogan would go through his clubs as though he were actually playing the golf course shot by shot.

One of today's great map makers is Tiger Woods. Before the 1997 Masters he reviewed films of previous

Masters tournaments to determine how the ball would break on the thirteenth green. He already knew that one pin placement would be near the front of the green, close to Rae's Creek, a placement that seemed to warrant an approach shot to the middle of the green. During the tournament, Woods had that exact putt, made an eagle, took the lead, and never looked back.

Whether it's preparing for the arduous Tour de France or the undulating greens at Augusta, the old axiom for success stated by Benjamin Franklin still stands true today: "When you fail to prepare, you are preparing to fail."

Build Muscle Memory
with Imagery

"Visualization. It may be the most important part of your mental package."[109]
—**Raymond Floyd**

A fascinating story about the mind-body connection involves Lieutenant John Dansfield and the powers of imagery. The lieutenant was captured during the Korean War and became a POW. His ace in the hole was that he loved golf. As a way to distract his mind, body, and soul from this dreadful time, Dansfield imagined playing his favorite golf course back in Topeka, Kansas. He would even visualize playing with his buddies, getting in at least five rounds of golf every day. He did this for all eighteen months of his imprisonment.

After the war ended, Dansfield returned to Topeka and made a beeline for his favorite golf course. Amazingly, when he picked up his clubs, he felt as if he had never left the game. In fact, Dansfield would tell friends that he actually felt that he was playing better than ever. Not only did imagery free his mind from the torment of his oppressors, but visualization helped him become a better golfer.

Imagery research has shown that such a mental exercise can help create and foster muscle memory. Imaging a task creates neural-motor connections in our body.[110] In the case of golf, when you imagine swinging a golf club, the muscles that you use for this activity will respond. You can't feel the muscles moving, but science tells us that the muscles are firing by assessing them with an electromyography (EMG) machine. The muscle activity involved in imagery is the same as actual performance, only to a smaller degree.

Muscle memory is a result of strengthening the neural-motor connections. By performing a task repetitively, neural pathways from the brain to the muscles are grooved. Over time, you no longer need to think about certain aspects of your swing. They just happen automatically due to the mus-

cle memory you have developed. Given that imagery produces slight forms of muscular activity, this type of mental
practice will help groove the neural pathways and create
muscle memory just like actual performance.

Of course, you can develop your muscle memory better by actually playing, but there are many opportunities in
which you may not be able to be on your favorite golf course.
Perhaps you live up North, where during the winter months
a few sessions a week of visualizing your swing can keep you
fresh. Ditto if you have a hectic workday schedule. Take
advantage of your breaktime or downtime at work and visualize making the swings you desire. Your muscles will love it.

45

Set Your Flame

"Each golfer has to understand his temperament before he can learn to manage it."

—Richard Coop

Tour golfer Brian Gay won the Southeastern Conference individual championship in both his sophomore and senior years. His dominance, however, was a mixed blessing. Following his first SEC victory, Gay performed very poorly his junior year, following a similar pattern of a terrible opening round and then two fairly good rounds.

Gay's problem was his motivation level. He apparently lost interest his junior year because he had already won their conference title. When he went to tournaments as a junior, his intensity was far too low in his first round and his scores showed it. However, he didn't want to finish near the bottom, so he would somehow reenergize himself for the last two rounds. His finishes were good, but not good enough.

It was recommended to Brian that he envision his practice round as his first round. He was to keep score and treat it exactly as if it were his first round of play. In this way, he would push his intensity level up a notch when he began his actual first round. This simple strategy worked. He finished in the top fifteen his next tournament and had a top-three finish in the following tournament.

Interestingly, another player on Gay's team had the reverse problem—this other player would play a great first and second round, then stumble in for the last round. His problem was that he was far too geared up for his last round. The advice given this other player was to employ an approach opposite to what had been prescribed for Gay. He was to treat his third round as if it were a practice round, toning down the intensity. As a result, Gay's teammate began to play exceptionally well all three rounds.

A useful analogy to understand this process is setting a flame on the stove for heating up soup. If the flame is set too low, the soup will take forever to cook. If the flame is set too high, the soup will come to a boil too quickly and perhaps burn or spill over the sides. To cook the soup most effectively, you need to set the flame at the appropriate level. In Gay's case, his flame was too low in the first round. On the other hand, his teammate's flame was excessively high in the third round.

If you are notorious for being a slow starter, your flame is set too low at the start of play. If you are an amateur and typically play one-round events, then you may need to have a pre-event routine that gets you fired up, perhaps by taking more time to practice.

If, however, you are a player who struggles to bring a good round into the barn, it may be that your flame is set too high. You could tone it down by practicing relaxation techniques. Another strategy is to decrease your focus on the outcome and focus more on the process, taking one shot at a time.

To play your best golf, find the appropriate setting for your internal flame.

46

Balance Your Life's Portfolio

"I think if you were going to base your whole life on what you do on the golf course, you are up for a lot of ups and downs." [111]

—Tom Lehman

Jack Nicklaus is more than just a great golfer. He is a husband, father, grandfather, and quite the business entrepreneur. The Golden Bear designs golf courses and has a clothing line, among other outside interests. Some critics in the past have suggested that those other pursuits have limited Nicklaus's playing and practicing schedule, and as a result, he may not have realized his full potential on the course. Most likely, however, the opposite is true. All of Nicklaus's outside interests enhanced his play and likely extended his career.

If you place all your ego eggs into the proverbial golf basket, you will have a greater tendency to get more stressed during important events. That is, if golf is your only outlet for self-esteem, then you have a greater need to demonstrate your competence in a positive way. And with a greater need to demonstrate your self-esteem comes greater anxiety.

Finding balance in your life and diversifying your interests can alleviate the incredible pressure of competitive golf. Outside interests such as photography, painting, or playing the guitar can nourish your self-esteem in many ways. When Nicklaus didn't have a great round or tournament, he would bounce back much quicker because he has so many outside interests that buffered the blow of playing poorly. Furthermore, Nicklaus has mentioned that his family activities and business interests provided getaways from golf that refreshed him and renewed his eagerness for competitive golf.[112]

The Swedish National Women's Team develops their talent based on a system of creating balance and keeping golf in perspective. Their training philosophy is to focus on the development of the human being, and in the long run, the results will follow.[113] Given the Swedish stars who have exploded on the LPGA tour, such as Annika Sorenstam, Liselotte Neumann, and Catrin Nilsmark, one cannot fault the importance of diversification.

Financial advisers will tell you that the safest bet with investing is to diversity your portfolio. Some advisers will recommend that you invest in mutual funds, a diverse group of stocks. The key to this investment strategy is that while some of the stocks may go down, the others will accrue, balancing your investment. Over time, your stocks should eventually accrue and you will have made a smart choice with a diversified portfolio.

Invest in many outside areas. Balance your life's portfolio with many meaningful and fulfilling activities, and your game should accrue in the long run.

Whistle while You Work

"Under pressure, one of the most important things I have to remember to do is breathe." [114]

—Curtis Strange

Fuzzy Zoeller whistles his way through work. Get within a hundred feet of him during a tournament round and see if you can guess that tune.

A little music can lighten your mood, lower your blood pressure, and take your mind off your troubles. What whistling does for Zoeller and others is keep them relaxed under pressure by helping them breathe better.

Under pressure, we have a tendency to breathe improperly. Our breathing becomes more shallow and hastened. In some instances, it may even stop entirely. This is nature's way of allowing us to hear intruders or predators. [115]

The consequence of shallow or subdued breathing is a reduction of oxygen to our muscles.[116] In turn, our muscles tighten up, and we might lose our ability to control our golf swing. Further, shallow breathing due to anxiety can restrict the blood flow to the extremities. When this occurs, we lose feel.[117] Further, if we don't breathe deeply during competition, our chances of choking increase significantly. Byron Nelson said that one of his keys to prevent choking was to breathe deeply and rhythmically.[118]

Whistling forces us to breathe deeply, using the diaphragm. When we whistle, air is forced out to make sound. Experts have even recommended to individuals with respiratory difficulties that they breathe as if they are whistling.[119]

Perhaps whistling is not your favorite pastime, or perhaps you never learned to whistle. Try humming a tune. Humming will also promote deep breathing.

Whether or not you have music in you, just make sure you keep breathing under pressure.

Try Easy:
The Sam Snead Approach

"Once you try, golf is the hardest game you'll ever play." [120]

—Roger Maltbie

We have all heard the old sport adage to success, "Just give 110 percent," right? Well, not so fast. Giving "all you have" may actually be detrimental to performance.

One of the more famous golf stories of trying too hard involved Arnold Palmer at the 1966 U.S. Open at the Olympic Club. Palmer led Billy Casper by seven strokes with just nine holes to go in the final round. But Palmer wanted more than just a second U.S. Open win: He wanted to break Ben Hogan's Open-scoring record of 276. Palmer forced the issue, stumbled badly, and eventually lost to Casper in a play-off.

Your sports performance might be enhanced if you give a little less and try easy. An interesting experimental test was conducted with Olympic runners using a try-easy mentality. In the first race, these runners were told to run at 90 percent effort in a short sprint. In a second race, they were told to give it 100 percent effort. To their amazement, they actually ran faster in the first race when they tried a little easier.[121]

Trying too hard will not only limit your foot speed on the track, it may also decrease your swing speed. Forcing the issue and giving all your energy can cause excessive muscle tension, slowing down your arm speed and trunk rotation. However, trying easy should promote a more relaxed feeling that helps to create a greater shoulder turn and faster arm speed. This relaxed feeling of trying easy can also add to the overall fluidity and rhythm of your swing, contributing to effortless power.

The poster boy for the try-easy approach in golf was Slammin' Sam Snead, who decades ago could bust 300-yard drives with minimal effort. Sam claimed that he always swung at 80 percent of his full capacity. While that helped him stay in balance, it also contributed to his powerful and flowing swing.

Besides giving you extra power, the try-easy mentality may also help you get out of a slumping pattern. Ken Venturi, former U.S. Open winner and TV golf commentator, once said, "You can't make good scores happen. You've got to let it happen."[122] Palmer would have done well to heed that advice in 1966 at the U.S. Open. Alas, he not only lost to Casper, he also missed Hogan's scoring record by two shots.

Annika's "54 Vision"

"It is a funny thing about life: If you refuse to accept anything but the best, you very often get it." [123]

—W. Somerset Maugham

Expectations are paradoxical. They can motivate an individual to create wondrous achievements, but expectations can also become a ceiling of limitation.

An interesting study conducted with golf professionals illustrates this paradoxical effect of expectations. This study investigated the percentages of putts made by professional golfers from varying locations. However, an additional factor was examined, whether the putt was for birdie or par. Amazingly, regardless of distance, the pros made more putts for par than they did for birdies.

One plausible explanation for this is that professionals expect they should be making no worse than par on every hole, and birdies are a bonus. Perhaps they grind harder and focus better over a ten-foot par putt than they do a birdie putt of the same length, fearing a bogey more than they desire a birdie. This type of belief system will definitely hinder their scoring potential.

Not all pros, however, believe pars are the standard by which to be judged. Annika Sorenstam, for example, learned an important mind-set from her training in Sweden under the tutelage of the golf coach Pia Nilsson, who promoted "a 54 vision."[124] Nilsson instilled in her players the premise that every hole was a birdie hole and that a score of 54 for a round of golf is possible (on a par-72 layout). That said, it's no real surprise that Sorenstam became the first woman to shoot 59 in an LPGA event. She is comfortable going extremely low because her expectations are that every hole is a possible birdie.

Of course, amateurs need to have more realistic expectations that will help promote their scoring potential, even if it doesn't come close to producing a 54 or 59. A golfer who consistently shoots in the 90s should expect to make at least a bogey on each hole. More experienced amateurs who can shoot in the eighties should begin to believe that par is possible on every hole. In that way, they will grind more when the putt is for par. Professionals and expert golfers, on the other hand, should follow Sorenstam's "54 vision" and believe that every hole is a potential birdie. With this scoring philosophy, they will feel much more at ease when they are going low and having the round of their life.

Prevent Paralysis
by Analysis

"A full mind is an empty baseball bat."

—Branch Rickey

A centipede and a worm were in a race. The centipede with all its legs could easily outwalk the wriggling worm. However, the worm was very smart. At the start of the race, the worm asked the centipede how it could possibly move all those legs in perfect order, one right after the other. As soon as the centipede thought about how to walk, all its legs got tangled together. The worm then wriggled past the frozen centipede to victory.[125]

Golfers can freeze up, just like the centipede, when they overthink and overanalyze their swing. A great example is Ralph Guldahl, who won the 1937 and 1938 U.S. Opens and the 1939 Masters. According to Paul Runyan, one of his contemporaries, Guldahl had unmatched control over the golf ball. Along came a publisher asking Guldahl to write an instructional golf book, *Groove Your Golf.* The problem was that the golf swing came very naturally to Guldahl: So when he started to write his book, he had to break down his swing piece by piece and analyze his every move. When the book was finished, so was his game.[126]

How did Guldahl ruin his play when he began to overanalyze it? Let's use a musical analogy to answer that. An expert pianist will tell you that his fingers respond to the music, moving beautifully to the melody as if dancing on the keyboard. Ask that pianist to focus on what the fingers are doing and the music gets disjointed. Swinging the golf club is no different. Once you start to overanalyze your swing, you focus on mechanics and lose rhythm and tempo. Your swing gets disjointed, almost paralyzed in motion.

To prevent paralysis by analysis, you must learn to respond to the target, rather than overanalyze your every movement. One way to accomplish this is by having a routine that enables you to react to the target. A great example of this is Davis Love III's putting routine. During his routine he looks twice at the target. But as he moves his head back on the second glance, he begins the backswing with his putter. This routine forces him to react to the target and not get overanalytical.

Develop a routine that allows you to react and respond, and you will begin to play beautiful music on the course.

51

Discover Your Gambling Strategy

"Far better it is to dare mighty things to win glorious triumphs, even though checkered by failure, than to rank with those poor spirits that neither enjoy much nor suffer much because they live in the gray twilight that knows not victory nor defeat." [127]

—**Teddy Roosevelt**

P hil Mickelson lives by the words spoken by Teddy Roosevelt. He lets it ride and plays for the big payoff of eagles and birdies at the cost of bogeys and perhaps doubles. Playing it safe doesn't often make its way into his vocabulary. That would be living in the gray twilight to him.

Many analysts criticize Mickelson's "going for broke" style. But they haven't convinced him to become someone he isn't. High-risk play energizes him. In that regard, he is no different from a sky diver, racecar driver, or bungee jumper.

Psychologists have shown that high-risk personality styles have low levels of serotonin, a neurotransmitter that helps the brain function. Having low serotonin is analogous to the brain's being a car that is idling in low gear. High-risk behavior stimulates the serotonin production in the brain of high-risk takers and this, literally, shifts their brain into high gear. Thus, the stimulation of high-risk situations is rewarding and these individuals gravitate toward this type of behavior.

Conversely, there are individuals who live and play much more conservatively. These people are low-risk takers and, most likely, have more serotonin in their brain than their high-risk counterparts. Low-risk individuals participating in precarious activities are analogous to an engine running too hot. They get overloaded, find it discomforting and, thus, avoid such behaviors.[128]

Tour players who let it ride and are high-stake gamblers include Greg Norman, Karrie Webb, Sergio Garcia, John Daly, and, in their younger years, Arnold Palmer and

Ray Floyd. Those players who hold their chips and play low-risk golf have included the likes of Jack Nicklaus, Nick Faldo, Annika Sorenstam, Davis Love III, and Hale Irwin.

Are you a high-risk taker? Ask yourself: *Do I like driving fast in the rain? Do I love roller coasters? Do I like downhill skiing? Do I shoot for all the tucked pins on the greens?* If you answered yes to any of these questions, your style is like Mickelson's and golf's other high-risk takers. In this case, your play and attitude on the course should fit your personality. Going for broke and trying to make as many birdies as you can is rewarding to you. Go for it and let it ride.

On the other hand, if roller coasters make you nauseous or if you prefer bunny runs to the black diamond slopes, then you are probably a low-risk taker. Playing for tucked pins may not be your preference, and you will probably feel uncomfortable just thinking such risky thoughts. Play for pars and shoot for the middle of the greens. Think of birdies as a bonus. Play conservatively, and you should have more fun and shoot better scores.

Break the Anxiety Habit

"One cannot remove anxiety only by arguing it away."[129]

—**Paul Tillich**

Bill Russell is regarded by many as the greatest *team* basketball player of all time. He won more championships than any other player. In his book *Russell Rules*, he mentioned how he always believed in his abilities and loved to play the game. Yet, interestingly, he was so nervous before every game that he would get sick and throw up. It wasn't due to inappropriate thinking. He had conditioned his body to be extremely nervous before every game he played.

The understanding of classical conditioning began almost a hundred years ago under the experiments of the Russian scientist, Pavlov. In his famous experiment with dogs, he paired the ringing of a bell with the presentation of food. Over time he found that he could remove the food and the ringing of a bell alone would produce saliva in the dog's mouth. Like the dogs in Pavlov's experiment, we tend to condition our bodies to react to certain stimuli. Hearing a siren triggers us to pull over to the curb. Thinking about a serene place like a meadow in the mountains can bring feelings of relaxation.

Unfortunately, we can also condition ourselves to have excessive anxiety before every tournament or a pressure-packed round. A few bad tournaments in a row may condition our bodies to react negatively to competition. Even if you are well prepared, you still may have an overwhelming sense of dread and nervousness before play. Your thoughts can be appropriate, but your body responds in an inappropriate way.

To change this cycle of negative physiology, the body must be reconditioned. One of the best methods is systematic desensitization. This technique has two main parts. In the first part, the golfer devises an anxiety hierarchy, a listing of scenes within one situation, starting from the least anxiety-provoking and ending with the most anxiety-provoking. Let's say a golfer is overcome with first-tee jitters. The list for this problem would include all scenes leading up to and including hitting the opening tee shot. More specifically, the list would include driving into the parking lot, getting the clubs out of the trunk, putting on the golf shoes, walking over to the range, hitting practice balls, walking to the first tee, and hitting the first tee shot.

The second part of this systematic desensitization is to visualize this anxiety hierarchy while in a relaxed state. In this way the golfer learns to associate relaxation with anxiety-provoking images, with the relaxation response being stronger than the anxiety response. Therefore, the pairing of the two will quiet the anxiety. Using this procedure for a few weeks prior to a tournament will recondition the golfer's body to feel less nervous at the opening hole.

We go to the range in hopes of conditioning our bodies to make a correct swing. We must also condition our bodies to respond to pressure in the most appropriate fashion.

Let the Concentration Flow

"Concentrating for four hours will wear you out mentally." [130]

—**Sergio Garcia**

Think of concentration as a reservoir of mental energy. To play your best, you must let your concentration flow when you are hitting your shot. However, if the flood gates are wide open and you focus intensely for an entire round, this reservoir may be emptied too soon. To conserve these mental resources, the flood gates must be opened only at the most appropriate times.

Therefore, it is vital to develop a routine that allows a player to release the flow of concentration in such a controlled manner that it can be turned off so that the reservoir of mental energy does not run dry. Given that the highest levels of concentration take time to accumulate, the routine should also allow the flow of concentration to build and crescendo at the most appropriate moment.

A concentration routine that effectively taps into your mental energy is composed of four levels. To enter each level, imagine a dial that releases the flow of concentration from the reservoir. As the dial is turned up, the concentration flow increases, and the golfer becomes more focused on the task. As described in MentalRule 18 ("Be Trigger Happy"), the golfer needs to devise a trigger (either a word or action) that will crank the dial up to the appropriate level. Moreover, the golfer should have a different trigger for each of the four levels.

The first level of concentration, "the fun zone," begins after you have struck the ball. At this level, the golfer is enjoying the trees, birds, or a good conversation. Here, your concentration dial would be set at the lowest level—one.

The next level, "the think zone," starts when the player arrives at the ball. Time to crank up the concentration flow to about a three on the dial. At this level, the golfer determines a shot strategy figuring in factors such as yardage, wind, and direction.

Next, the golfer enters "the feel zone," where the concentration flow is turned up to a seven. The player is now focused on *feeling* the shot that must be executed. For instance, if the shot requires a fade, the player is taking practice swings that promote this feeling.

That brings the golfer to "the go zone." The floodgates of concentration are wide open. Concentration is now surging and the dial is set at the highest level—ten. After the shot has been executed and then analyzed, the player's concentration returns to the lowest level. The player is back to the fun zone and should be enjoying the walk to the ball. The concentration routine starts all over again and is repeated throughout the round.

54

Leap Over Your Plateaus

"Learning is like rowing upstream: not to advance is to drop back."
—**Chinese proverb**

One of golf's great joys is in advancing your skill level. Improvement breeds interest, and interest in turn promotes improvement.

The learning trail, however, inevitably involves many plateaus. You might see vast improvement at first, then plateau for a period. A little later you experience a little more improvement, then again hit the wall.

The learning cycle in golf, with its ups and downs, has many parallels to the principles of muscle building. When we lift weights, we place stress on our muscles. As an adaptive response to counteract this overload, the muscles produce more protein, thus stimulating an increase in muscle fibers.[131] Our muscles will stop growing unless they are continually overloaded. To experience muscle growth, you can add more weight to your routine, add more repetitions, and/or change your exercises.

Just as our muscles respond to overload, we will see improvement in our golf swing if we add new variables to the learning equation. This will force our bodies to adapt, making our swing grow beyond the current plateau. One variable that you might change is your equipment or your instructor, or you could start playing a new, more difficult course.

Stephen Jay Gould, author of *Ever Since Darwin*, explained evolution as a cycle of big leaps followed by plateaus. According to Gould, the big leaps are created by catastrophic events, such as great climatic variations. These events cause our species to adapt and then evolve. To have your golf swing continually evolve, do not place your swing under catastrophic events. Just add enough variations so that you may leap over your plateaus.

The Best Are
Never Satisfied

"It takes all the running you can do to keep up in the same place. If you want to get somewhere else, you must run at least twice as fast as you can."
—the **Queen of Hearts** in *Alice in Wonderland*

Socrates was credited with being one of the smartest men of his time. When he was asked what made him stand out among great men of philosophical wisdom, he replied, "My wisdom lay in this: unlike other men, I know how ignorant I am."[132]

Basketball great Larry Bird followed this philosophy throughout his career. Although Bird was incredibly talented in many areas, he knew he had to keep improving. He said, "If I don't keep changing, I'm history. I work hard all the time. I've always been willing to learn and get better."[133]

Jack Nicklaus, voted as the greatest player of the twentieth century, holds a belief similar to Bird's. For example, he learned a new wrinkle to his short game just before the 1986 Masters (which he won) thanks to a tip from Chi Chi Rodriguez. Interestingly, this tip was relayed to Jack through his caddie and son, Jackie.[134] You would think a guy in his forties would be satisfied with his skills, but the best are never satisfied. Such an attitude kept Nicklaus on top of the golfing world for so many years.

Tiger Woods is another who is never content with his playing level. Although Woods won his first major, the 1997 Masters, by twelve strokes, he believed that his swing was too long and his clubface was too shut at the top. He could not hit the soft flowing shots he would need to win the other majors. As a result, he and his swing coach, Butch Harmon, went to work and revamped his swing.

Annika Sorenstam is also on a quest to improve her game. She and her coach write an evaluation after each tournament, outlining what was good about the round and what could have been better.[135] Even after her second U.S. Open victory, by eight strokes this time, she was concerned about getting her evaluation from her coach so she could get better for the next major.

When we become complacent with our abilities, we stop growing and achieving. There is an old African parable that describes how we all must keep progressing in our lives:

> Every morning in Africa, the gazelle wakes up and knows it must run faster than the fastest lion.
>
> Every morning, a lion wakes up and knows it must outrun the slowest gazelle or it will starve.
>
> It does not matter whether you are a gazelle or a lion,
>
> When the sun comes up, you better start running.

If you want to continually improve yourself, you'd better lace up the shoes and start working on the game.

56

Create Positive Superstitions

"Superstition is the poetry of life."

—Goethe

Superstitions exist in all walks of life. We avoid the number 13. We don't walk under ladders, and we try not to break any mirrors.

Golf is no exception when it comes to superstitions. Chi Chi Rodriguez marks his ball with the head side up, and he never uses pennies.[136] Then there's Ben Crenshaw, who's been known to play only low-numbered balls, one through four, because he doesn't want to make a score higher than that.[137]

Why do people have such superstitions? The principle of intermittent reinforcement can help resolve this mystery.

Tommy Armour III uses a 1969 dime to mark his ball.[138] Armour might forget all the times he has putted poorly with that coin, but given that he will putt well every once in a while using it, his superstitious behavior is reinforced and stays in his repertoire.

While these behaviors may seem strange, they provide peace of mind. Golf, like all sports, is very unpredictable. Golfers are trying to gain some control over the outcome of an event, and superstitions provide a sense of control. If they follow this behavior, they believe that their play will be enhanced. Would any sport psychologist recommend such habits? Of course, as long as they are not counterproductive or inappropriate, such as skipping breakfast because you played well the one time you did.

More important, you should develop positive superstitions, such as the belief that you must practice your putting for ten minutes before every round.

Practice with a
Shag Mentality

"It isn't the hours you put in at practice that count. It's the way you spend those minutes." [139]

—**Tony Lema**

In the old days, the golf range was practically nonexistent. Pros had to shag their own balls, hitting them into a field and then going to pick them up. While this is far from convenient by today's standards, it may actually be the best way to practice your golf skills.

Ben Hogan would hit about twenty balls and then take a break. Given his penchant for precision, he must have discovered through trial and error that this was the best way for him to practice. Psychologists have discovered that when practicing a discrete motor skill such as hitting golf balls, learning is enhanced when you practice in a distributed schedule, which is when practice time and break time are approximately equal. In a distributed schedule, you would hit balls for ten minutes and then rest for ten minutes.[140]

When you shag (and, please, no Austin Powers jokes here), there is the downtime of picking up the balls in the field. During this time, the golfer can analyze and process what was just learned. And when swing information is processed more deeply, it will be remembered better.

Shagging balls, unfortunately, is a lost art. What typically occurs nowadays is that an amateur gets a big bucket of a hundred balls, hits them all in succession, and takes little or no breaks between swings. With this type of practice regime, there is little processing going on; as a result, the mind and body will absorb very little.

Furthermore, learning diminishes greatly when we are tired. Unless you are in superb shape, hitting that many balls is extremely tiring on the mind and the body.

Okay, so you still aren't ready to leave the luxury of a practice range. Fine. But at least you can go to the range with a *shag mentality*. Hit balls for ten minutes, then sit down for ten minutes and think about your swing. Gary Player suggests that golfers would be better served if they kept their range balls some distance away. With this strategy, they are forced to take some time and process each swing between shots.[141]

While practicing with a shag mentality may slow you down, it will speed up the learning process.

58

Develop More Brainpower in Your Game

"An active mind cannot exist in an inactive body." [142]

—**Gen. George S. Patton**

The golf world has discovered the importance of keeping the body in shape. Players like Tiger Woods and David Duval work out regularly. Compare Duval's frumpy physique of five years ago with his Adonis-like body of today. He lost about twenty pounds in fat, but gained it all back in muscle.

But it is more than just the top players. Professionals from all the tours are working out with weights and running miles to develop their cardiovascular endurance. The hope is that the enhanced muscular strength will not only allow them to hit the ball farther, but also promote the ability to control the clubface when the ball finds the high rough. The cardiovascular workouts will also help by keeping the legs fresh throughout eighteen holes or longer, if necessary.

Researchers also have found that being in shape helps the mind function better. Individuals who exercise regularly make better decisions. A healthy body also increases the level of concentration and alertness. Staying in shape can also promote creative thought. Exercise, then, can help you visualize better on the course.[143]

Science offers an easy explanation for all this. When you work out with weights and participate in cardiovascular activities, the heart gets stronger. A strengthened heart can pump more nutrients and oxygen to all the tissues and organs, including the brain. Thus, when you are in better shape, your brain will work that much better.

While the mind controls the body, the body also affects the mind. Work out. You will have more brainpower for your game.

Be Flexible in Your Attentional Style

"Your planning tool should be your servant, never your master."
—**Stephen Covey**

The San Francisco 49ers were an incredible team for most of the eighties and nineties, winning four Super Bowls thanks in large part to quarterbacks Joe Montana and Steve Young. While both were highly successful, they had very different styles. Montana commanded his forces like a general marching down the gridiron. His style was to stick with his plan and hold fort in the pocket, even when 300-pound linemen were about to pounce. Young was more the matador, reacting to would-be tacklers as if they were charging bulls. When the pressure was on, he would scramble out of the pocket and create plays.

Montana's and Young's attentional styles characterized their distinctive play. An attentional style is defined as a mode to process information within the environment. According to sport psychologists, individuals can have four different modes of attention: the reactor, the spotter, the planner, and the internalizer.[144] A golfer in the reactor mode focuses on surroundings such as wind. A golfer in the spotter mode concentrates on one specific aspect of the environment, such as the back of the golf ball. A golfer in the planner mode focuses on devising a strategy for the hole, such as hitting an eight-iron to the middle of the green. The internalizer mode focuses on physiological factors, such as heart rate or sweaty palms.

On any one golf shot, a golfer will tap into all four attentional styles. The focus might first be on outside factors such as how strong the wind is blowing (the reactor). Then a decision is made to hit a six-iron given the strength of the wind (the planner). Then at the start of your routine, you might take a deep breath and get rid of your nervousness (the internalizer). Then your focus might shift to a dimple on the ball (the spotter).

Be Flexible in Your Attentional Style

Here's the rub: When under pressure, you will go to the mode most comfortable for you. Which is your style in golf? If it is similar to Joe Montana's and the pressure is on, you might stick with the plan and disregard the wind changes and end up using the wrong club for the situation. If you are like Steve Young and in the heat of competition, you might react to a sudden gust of wind and change your plan in the middle of your swing. In that case, you will be less committed to your shot, and commitment to the shot is essential.

The key to playing your best golf is to be flexible in your attentional style. Davis Love III has said that he has a plan for each hole and what club he wants to hit off each tee, where he wants to hit his approach, and whether he wants to go for the par-fives in two or not. The key to Love's plan is that he alters it given the conditions of the course.[145] Love realizes flexibility is vital to success on the golf course.

Be a planner like Montana, but also have the flexibility to react like Young when necessary. In that way, you may be able to shoot more "SanFrantastic" scores.

Excellence Has Its Price

"Those who win at something have no real advantage over you because they had to pay the price for the reward." [146]

—Epictetus

Do you envy how John Daly can blast his drives 350 yards? Do you wish you possessed Phil Mickelson's incredible touch around the greens or Brad Faxon's beautiful putting stroke?

Excellence has its price. Early in his career Greg Norman would get up at the crack of dawn and beat balls until his hands bled. [147] Nick Faldo left college after his first semester because his teammates were having too much fun and not taking their practice or game seriously. Mac O'Grady tried and failed the PGA Tour's Q-school seventeen times before he finally succeeded.

Amateurs who attain a high level of expertise also have paid the price. The long hours on the range or putting green that were spent to become a single-digit handicap took precious time away from family, friends, and business.

We typically see in others like Norman and Faldo only the end point in their journeys to excellence, not their tribulations. Appreciate that the attainment of expertise is not given freely—a rule not just for the golf course, but for all walks of life.

Find Your Purpose

"What other people find in poetry or art museums, I find in the flight of a good drive: the white ball sailing up into the blue sky, reaching its apex, falling and finally dropping to the turf, just the way I planned it." [148]

—Arnold Palmer

G*olf in the Kingdom*, a best-selling novel about the spirituality of golf, offers the story about a student who plays a magical round of golf in Scotland. Most of the action takes place one night and is about the mentoring of the student around the course by a mystical caddie named Shivas Irons. Michael Murphy, the author and follower of Eastern philosophies, illustrates that golf can be a vehicle for human growth. Golf sets us on a path of self-examination and also gives us a life direction when perhaps there is none.

Hal Sutton's kingdom is the golf course, but for a while he lost his crown. He was touted as the next Jack Nicklaus in the early eighties. He was a good-looking kid in his early twenties with a serious demeanor mature beyond his years, and he had the talent to match. In his first five years on the PGA Tour, Sutton registered seven victories, including the Tournament of Champions as well as a win at the PGA Championship, where he outdueled Nicklaus. With all that success came money, fame, and heightened expectations.

By the early nineties, Sutton's game and mind-set had fallen into a dungeon of despair. His swing was lost amid a state of confusion. He fired his longtime coach, Jimmy Ballard, and ditched his long-term caddie. Sutton nearly lost his tour playing privileges, and by 1993 he had hit rock bottom. Golf then gave Sutton a more precious lesson than money or fame could ever buy, and it came right out of *Golf in the Kingdom*: The game forced Sutton to reexamine himself. He worked his way back by following a path of self-discovery that led to his questioning of his ideals and values.[149]

Sutton finally discovered what his purpose was on the golf course. It was not for money; it was for pride and for the love of the game. With this new self-awareness, he began his ascension back to the top ranks in the game. By the late nineties, he was again a top player on the PGA Tour. He started winning tournaments again, at one point outdueling Tiger Woods to win the Players Championship.

Finding meaning enables you to tap into inner strengths, resources, abilities, and energies that you did not know existed. In *C Zone*, Robert Kreigel interviewed five hundred top performers from all areas of business, creative arts, and sports, and he discovered they all had a purpose and were passionate about that purpose. Kreigel has written that a meaningful purpose is the single most important quality that will lift a person head and shoulders above the rest in tough times. It brings the whole being into play and centers your energy toward overcoming any arduous task.

Once you find your meaning, develop an attitude and practice schedule that fits this purpose. If it is to be with friends, then make sure you enjoy the walk. If it is to be with nature, then make sure you smell the flowers along the way. If it is for recognition and money, start pounding balls.

Notes

1. Carnegie, Dale, *How to Win Friends and Influence People*. New York: Simon & Schuster, 1937.

2. Riley, Pat, *The Winner Within*. New York: Berkeley Publishing Group, 1994.

3. Robbins, Anthony, *Awaken the Giant Within*. New York: Fireside, 1991.

4. Riach, Steve, *It Is How You Play the Game: Faith, Courage, and Determination through Every Round of Golf*. Tulsa, OK: Honor Books, 2001.

5. Edell, Dean, *Eat Drink and Be Merry*. New York: HarperCollins, 1999.

6. Robbins.

7. Csikszentmihaly, Mihaly, *Flow: The Psychology of Optimal Experience*. New York: Harper Perennial, 1990.

8. *Los Angeles Times*, July 15, 2002.

9. *Golf Magazine*, January 2000.

10. Robbins.

11. *Golf Magazine*, July 1998.

12. Irwin, Hale, *Hale Irwin's Smart Golf*. New York: HarperCollins Publishers, 2001.

13. Lowe, Janet, *Michael Jordan Speaks*. New York: John Wiley & Sons, 1999.

14. Freeman, Criswell, *The Golfer's Book of Wisdom*. Nashville, TN: Walnut Grove Press, 1995.

15. Wade, Don, *And Then Justin told Sergio*. Chicago, IL: Contemporary Books, 2002.

16. *Golf Digest*, May 1996.

17. Millman, Dan, *Everyday Enlightenment: 12 Gateways to Personal Growth*. New York: AOL Time Warner Book Group, 1998.

18. Woods, Tiger, *How I Play the Game*. New York: Warner Books, 2001.

19. Gelb, Michael J., *Discover Your Genius*. New York: HarperCollins, 2001.

20. *Golf Magazine*, March 2001.

21. Wiren, Gary, and Richard Coop, *The New Golf Mind*. New York: Simon & Schuster, 1985.

22. Ballesteros, Seve, and John Andrisani, *Seve Ballesteros: Natural Golf*. New York: Macmillan Publishing, 1988.

23. Gelb.

24. Coop, Richard, *Mind over Golf*. New York: Simon & Schuster, 1993.

25. *Golf Magazine*, January 1999.

26. *Golf Digest*, June 1997.

27. *Golf Digest*, September 1996.

28. Bull, Stephen, John Albinson, and Christopher Shambrook, *Mental Game Plan*. Morgantown, WV: Fitness Information Technology, 1999.

29. Player, Gary, *The Golfer's Guide to the Meaning of Life: Lessons I've Learned from My Life on the Links*. Emmaus, PA: Rodale: St. Martin's Press, 2001.

30. Dorfman, H. A., *Mental Game of Baseball*. South Bend, IN: Diamond Communications, 1989.

31. Film at Louisville Slugger in Louisville, KY.

32. Nicklaus, Jack, and Ken Bowden, *Jack Nicklaus: My Story*. New York: Simon & Schuster, 1997.

33. Love, Davis III, *Every Shot I Take*. New York: Simon & Schuster, 1997.

34. *Golf Magazine*, June 2001.

35. Rotella, Bob, *Golf is Not a Game of Perfect*. New York: Simon & Schuster, 1995.

36. Dyer, Wayne, *The Sky's the Limit*. New York: Simon & Schuster, 1980.

37. Bradley, Jon, *Quotable Byron*. Nashville, TN: TowleHouse Publishing, 2002.

38. Player.

39. Pintor, S., *How the Brain Works*. New York: Norton, 1997.

40. Andrisani, John, *Think Like Tiger*. New York: Penguin Putnam, 2002.

41. *Golf Magazine*, June 2001.

42. Player.

43. *Golf World*, January 11, 2002.

44. *Golf Magazine*, April 1997.

45. *Golf Digest*, June 1997.

46. Gould, Dan, and Robert Weinberg, *The Foundations of Sport and Exercise Psychology*. Champaign, IL: Human Kinetics, 2000.

47. Steinberg, Gregg, Shane Frehlich, and Keith Tennant, *Perceptual Motor Skills*, 1995.

48. Robbins.

49. Andrisani.

50. Voorhees, Randy, *As Hogan Said: The 389 Best Things Ever Said about How to Play Golf*. New York: Simon & Schuster, 2000.

51. Robbins.

52. Orlick, Terry, *In Pursuit of Excellence*. Champaign, IL: Human Kinetics, 1990.

53. *Golf Digest*, May 1997.

54. Wade, *And Then Justin told Sergio*.

Notes

55. Maxwell, John, *Failing Forward*. Nashville, TN: Thomas Nelson Publishers, 2000.

56. Riach.

57. Shapiro, Alan, *Golf's Mental Hazards*. New York: Simon & Schuster, 1996.

58. Dorfman.

59. Rotella.

60. *Golf Digest*, March 1997.

61. Csikszentmihaly, Mihaly, *Creativity:The Work & Lives of 91 Eminent People*. New York: HarperCollins, 1996.

62. Wade, Don, *And Then Tiger Told the Shark*. Chicago: Contemporary Books, 1998.

63. Rotella.

64. Robbins.

65. Maxwell.

66. *Golf Magazine*, September 1990.

67. *Golf Digest*, January 1997.

68. Cohen, Patrick, *Going Low*. New York: McGraw-Hill: Contemporary, 2002.

69. *Golf Digest*, May 2002.

70. Graham, Deborah, *Eight Traits of Championship Golfers*. New York: Simon & Schuster, 1999.

71. *Golf Digest*, March 1996.

72. Voorhees.

73. Nicklaus and Bowden.

74. Shapiro.

75. Wade, Don, *And Then Jack Said to Arnie*. Chicago: Contemporary Books, 1991.

76. *Golf Digest*, June 1995.

77. Gardner, Howard, *Extraordinary Minds*. New York: HarperCollins, 1997.

78. Bull, Albinson, and Shambrook.

79. Gardner.

80. Dorfman.

81. *Ultimate Athlete*. New York: Discovery Communications, 1996.

82. Wade, *And Then Justin Told Sergio*.

83. *T &L Golf*, March/April 2002.

84. Kushner, Howard, *When Everything You Wanted Isn't Enough*. New York: Simon & Schuster, 1986.

85. Graham.

86. Gould and Weinberg.

87. Wade, *And Then Justin Told Sergio*.

88. Csikszentmihaly, *Flow*.

89. *Golf Digest*, May 1995.

90. Coop.

91. Freeman.

92. *Golf Digest*, March 2001.

93. Schmidt, Richard, and Craig Wrisberg, *Motor Learning and Performance*. Champaign, IL: Human Kinetics, 2000.

MentalRules® for Golf

94. *Golf Magazine*, June 2002.

95. *Mid-south Golfer*, April 2002.

96. *Golf Magazine*, April 2002.

97. Rotella.

98. Millman.

99. Wade, *And Then Shark Told Justin*.

100. Sorbel, D. S., and R. Ornstein, *Good Humor, Good Health*, www. Kaiserpermanente.org.

101. Freeman.

102. *Psychological Review*, 16, 1994.

103. *International Journal of Sport Psychology*, 19, 1988.

104. Kriegel, Robert, *If It Ain't Broke, Break It*. New York: Warner Books, 1991.

105. Parent, Joseph, *Zen Golf*. New York: Doubleday, 2002.

106. Voorhees.

107. Armstrong, Lance, with Sally Jenkins, *It's Not About the Bike*. New York: Penguin Putnam, 2000.

108. Andrisani.

109. Bull, Albinson, and Shambrook.

110. Schmidt and Wrisberg.

111. Coop.

112. *Golf Magazine*, April 1996.

113. *Golf Digest*, December 1996.

114. Shapiro.

115. Parent.

116. Shapiro.

117. Parent.

118. Bradley.

119. Spurlock, Jeanne, American Medical Women's Association, www.amwa-doc.org/publications/WCHeal thbook/stressamwa-cho9.html. page 6.

120. Wade, *And Then Jack Said to Arnie*.

121. Lynch, Jerry, *Thinking Mind: Dancing Mind*. New York: Bantam Books, 1992.

122. Jones, Charlie, and Kim Doren, *Be the Ball*. Kansas City, MO: Andrews McNeel Publishing, 2000.

123. Millman.

124. Nilsson, Pia, GolfOnline.

125. Parent.

126. *Golf Digest*, May 1999.

127. Orlick.

128. *The Addicted Brain*. Princeton, NJ: Films for the Humanities and Sciences, 1990.

129. Tillich, Paul, *The Courage to Be*. New Haven, CT: Yale University Press, 1952.

130. *Golf Magazine*, June 2001.

131. Insel, Paul, and Walton Roth, *Core Concepts in Health*. Boston: McGraw-Hill, 2002.

132. Robbins.

Notes

133. Kriegel.

134. Hall, Jay, *The Executive Trap*. New York: Simon and Schuster, 1992.

135. *Golf Digest*, June 1997.

136. Wade, *And Then Tiger Told the Shark*.

137. *Golf Magazine*, October 1989.

138. Ibid.

139. Voorhees.

140. Schmidt and Wrisberg.

141. Player.

142. Van Ekeren, Glen, *Speaker's Sourcebook II*. New York: Prentice Hall Press, 2002.

143. Insel and Roth.

144. Gould and Weinberg.

145. *Golf Digest*, February 1998.

146. Lebell, Sharon, *Epictetus: The Art of Living: A New Interpretation*. New York: HarperCollins, 1995.

147. *Golf Digest*, May 1995.

148. *Golf Magazine*, May 1996.

149. Ibid., August 1995.